TO B&B OR NOT TO B&B

TO B&B OR NOT TO B&B

By Sue Marko

HOW MY DREAM LODGE BECAME A COMEDIC NIGHTMARE

◆ FriesenPress

One Printers Way
Altona, MB R0G 0B0
Canada

www.friesenpress.com

Copyright © 2025 by Sue Marko
First Edition — 2025

All rights reserved.

No part of this publication may be reproduced in any form, or by any means, electronic or mechanical, including photocopying, recording, or any information browsing, storage, or retrieval system, without permission in writing from FriesenPress.

ISBN
978-1-03-835022-0 (Hardcover)
978-1-03-835021-3 (Paperback)
978-1-03-835023-7 (eBook)

1. HUMOR, TOPIC, BUSINESS & PROFESSIONAL

Distributed to the trade by The Ingram Book Company

This book never would have come to be without two parents who accepted my unconventional life path. They disagreed with my decision to open a B&B but supported me and talked me off the ledge when things went sideways. Thank you, with much love, to my Mom and Dad!

I'd also like to take the opportunity to acknowledge and say a big 'Thank You" to the many wonderful guests that I had through the years, some of whom I became friends with and I'll be blessed to stay in touch with them always. They know who they are.... they're not in this book.

Table of Contents

Chapter 1 - Where It All Began — 1

Chapter 2 - Buying the B&B — 5

Chapter 3 - Allergies — 25

Chapter 4 - There's No Way Your Mom Taught You That — 39

Chapter 5 - Damage — 67

Chapter 6 - Why Are You Not at a Hotel? — 79

Chapter 7 - The Assholes — 95

Chapter 8 - Outside Forces — 141

Chapter 9 - Reviews — 187

Chapter 10 - Reservations Required — 197

Chapter 11 - Selling the B&B — 205

About the Author — 223

Chapter 1 - Where It All Began

I remember the first time I ever stayed in a B&B; it was on San Juan Island for my youngest brother's wedding. It was run by a couple, these two guys who really were the hosts with the most. Their place was immaculately decorated and it was in a beautiful area, a stone's throw from the ocean where the yachts in the marina were lined up, oozing of wealth, decadence, and the life of total luxury and happiness that we all dream of living. The guys were always smiling, they were kind, friendly, and full of suggestions for touring their resort town as they presented us with delicious fresh-baked treats every morning. But what really struck me was how peaceful and happy they were; it was like their lives were perfect and they knew it. That may have been where I was infected by the bug that would cause me to follow that same path toward creating that same perfect life, along with evoking that same sense of awe in others that they created in me.

Like myself, you may have stayed at a place like this and thought "I'm a great host and an awesome cook and my breakfasts would be the best my guests ever tasted! My guests would be so wowed and so grateful that I would always feel so appreciated and satisfied with a feeling of total *winning*!" After a while, the draw becomes overwhelming as you ask yourself over and over again, "To B&B or not to B&B?"

That, truly, is the question! And I hope to give you some insight into the answer that is best for you if you are considering becoming the host or hostess of a Bed and Breakfast yourself. There are so many things that can make or break your business that are completely out of your hands—things that suddenly pop up—and you might be able to conquer them, but you might not. It's not my intent to scare you away from the dream, but I hope to enlighten you to the nightmarish dark little corners that you haven't thought much about, perhaps because you didn't even know they existed… like how I didn't know either.

I sold my house that was in a great neighborhood near all of my friends and family to pull money together towards a deposit, legal fees, furniture, and a million other start-up costs. I quit my job (much to everyone's horror) which brought in a good salary with every possible employee benefit, to answer my calling to self-employment and what I thought would be freedom and independence. Fourteen years later, when I sold the property and could leave, was the only time since buying it that I started to feel free and independent once more.

About the time I listed the lodge "For Sale" was when I started to write down the many stories ahead that comprise this book. I had been through so much in what was then around six years into the project, that I just wanted to move on; to put all of the past behind me and once again start a new life filled with optimism and adventure. The fantasy of the big log lodge in the middle of the mountains had begun to fade out into something much less romantic, and I was already beginning to resent it. I was sick of the public coming into my home and disrespecting both it and me. I was sick of their demands, their habits, their weird body noises and smells, their hairs in sinks, on the toilet seats and in the shower, their spills and messes, their stupid jokes, their drama, their bullshit, and their presence in my life. Some of the things that guests would do appalled me; I could not believe some of the crap they pulled and I found the best way to really vent was to proverbially puke it all out onto paper... it was the only way I was able to process and move on from their horrendous evils! I thought back to the beginning and recalled the choice moments that needed to be eternalized in print and began my road of personal therapy by resurrecting the good, the bad, and the ugly—including those assholes who caused me to lose sleep, question my own abilities, or who just simply insulted the hell out me. Yes, it was definitely time to get out! Too bad it would be another eight years before that would happen and the lodge would finally sell.

One of my favorite movies of all time is *Out of Africa*. In the opening scene, as the camera scans the awesome African savannah, the Baroness says, "I once owned a farm in Africa." Her voice is solemn, reflective, and a bit sad as she recalls the great joys, the astronomical losses, and the terrible injustices that she suffered over many years all in that one short statement. Today, I feel like there are many parallels between the Baroness' story and mine, the biggest difference being that mine is told (mostly) with a smile, to recall the events with as much humour as can be derived and maintaining my eternal gratefulness to the Powers That Be that got me the hell out of there before all sanity was lost.

· · · · ·

Chapter 2 - Buying the B&B

TR, who was my boyfriend and business partner at the time, and I looked at a lot of properties and homes to begin our B&B. In the end, the one we both really wanted wasn't on the market; the realtor had known that the owners were looking to sell, so a deal came to happen. The actual transfer seemed normal enough at first, but that soon changed.

The owners claimed to have used it occasionally as a Bed & Breakfast, but they had no business records and never had operated at a professional level. There was no branding, no advertising, no capacity for credit card payments, no health board certification, no guest postings anywhere, and no hot tub for winter clientele. It was their house that they lived in, and they had casually rented out a couple of rooms to a couple of people here and there. So, we purchased it like any home purchase, and we expected to furnish it and begin the real business ourselves. They had promised us their customer list on possession, but strangely, it never materialized; my suspicion was that it never really existed.

Prior to possession of the property (November, 2002), I got a call from the husband asking me if I would pay for a load of firewood that he had ordered earlier that fall. The house had a wood-burning furnace, so firewood was about to become a giant part of my life if I wanted to heat the place. I asked him how much it was, and he told me $600. I told him I thought that was a bit steep for a load of firewood and he explained to me that it was a whole flipping logging truck full, not a pick-up truck! Having no experience with logging trucks other than avoiding colliding with them on the highway, I had no idea how big that was, but I knew it had to be VERY big, so I agreed and sent him the money. So here I was, picturing an enormous pile of perfectly chopped up firewood that would last and last for several winters. When we took possession, to my shock there were around thirty-five seventy-foot logs (uncut) varying in thickness lying on the lawn at least 400 feet from where the wood chute was. This ridiculous monstrosity turned out to cost me a bundle of time and money to deal with. As I discovered in the following years it would have been simpler, way less of a mess, and much less expensive to simply hire a guy to bring it already cut up in his pick-up load by load. Why do people create filthy and incredibly hard work for themselves? What the hell are they thinking? And is this rambling pile of full-length logs really what you think your guests who pay to stay in your home want to look at? *Dorothy, you're so not in Kansas anymore!* And now, you have a big mess in your front yard that ALL of your guests are going to see.

We took possession on November 30. As would turn out to be the case with almost everything to do with the property and the business, TR would not be available for the possession, so I convinced a really great friend of mine to make the move with me. We arrived late at night on the 30th; the moving truck was arriving first thing the following morning, so we drove into the late-night hours in order to be there when most of my worldly possessions would join me. We had all my plants, jewelry, a couple of overnight bags, sleeping bags (there would be beds in the guest rooms but no linens), my entire collection of wine (which was many, many cases) with a sleeve of plastic cups, and my beloved golden retriever with us in our two vehicles.

The house was dark, with not even the porch light on, so we had a bit of drama seeing our way in. Thankfully, as arranged with the realtor, the door was unlocked so at least we didn't have to fumble with keys in the dark. When we got in, we turned some lights on and immediately opened a bottle of wine that we were really ready for after the long drive from another province. As we surveyed the room, we realized they hadn't finished moving; there was still some furniture and packed up boxes in the living room! My moving van was arriving at 10:00 a.m., so we briefly debated whether or not we should move the items to the porch area to make room for all my stuff. While we were chatting, we heard a noise from one of the guest bedrooms. My dog jumped to attention and let out a warning bark. My friend and I were startled and decided to see what the noise was, so we tiptoed down the hall, opened the door, and flicked on the light to see the husband getting up from a bed where his wife lay... and both were totally naked!

Everyone shrieked at once and my friend and I pulled the door shut, stammering an "Oh my God, I'm so sorry!" while my dog continued barking. My friend and I looked at each other and burst out laughing on our way back to the kitchen. "What are they doing here?!" we couldn't believe it as we double-checked the date with ourselves to make sure we weren't a day early. Nope, it was November 30, and it was my house, and they were still in it, and we saw them naked! Wow, who expects that when you move in?! I could hear the theme from the *Twilight Zone* playing over and over in my head. More wine, please!

In shock, we sat at the kitchen bar to consume some wine and make sense of what was happening. A few minutes passed and the husband and wife emerged from the bedroom (dressed, thank God!). As we poured them a glass of wine, they gave us some story about the house that they bought not being ready and that they and their remaining items would be out of the house first thing in the morning. I said that would be great because my moving truck would be there around the same time and I would need all of their things to be gone by then.

Suddenly the other bedroom door opened and their teenaged daughter and a middle-aged woman whom I had not met before came out in their pajamas. The woman would turn out to be an aunt, either the sister of the husband of the wife; I didn't soak up the details of the family tree that was sleeping in my house. They all settled into the wine we had brought in and stayed up pounding it back until around 3:00 a.m.

As an aside, years later I was chatting with the friend who helped me move and we were reminiscing about that November 30 move and how "Twilight Zone" it was. She asked me if I remembered the HAIR sweater; apparently someone was wearing some sweater that looked like it was made out of human hair! Fortunately, I have blocked that out and don't remember it at all, but she is still plagued by the memory and quite grossed out by it (no kidding, so gross!). I guess she hasn't had a suitable replacement memory for that one yet.

I have a theory that your head is only so big, which means your brain is only so big, and in turn, the piece responsible for memory storage is only so big, and each memory is both a very definable size and of a very definite category. Because of maximum capacity restrictions, sometimes, if something needs to go (there can be many reasons rooted in psychology for this need) and something of the same size and suitability comes along, there is a replacement and a disposal of the old one. My theory neatly explains that either my friend doesn't need to dispose of the memory of the hair-sweater yet or she hasn't yet experienced the appropriately replacement memory. Apparently, I needed to get rid of that one, and I'm glad I succeeded in doing so, but the bad news is that it was likely replaced with something of equal repulsiveness; maybe even something that is recounted later in this book.

Back to the story...

While we practiced the fine art of small talk, it occurred to me that since both guest rooms were taken, my friend and I had nowhere to sleep; all of my beds were in the moving truck along with couches, etc. I voiced this concern and the wife informed us that she had a mattress in the garage, and we could move it to the master bedroom upstairs for me and my friend to sleep on. How thoughtful—the first night in my new home, and I get to share a mattress from the garage (spider-haven!) on the floor while this clan of squatters all enjoyed what were now my beds with real box springs and frames!

After several bottles of wine, we decided it was time to get some sleep. My friend and I picked up our small amount of luggage and our sleeping bags and headed up to the master suite to check out our sleeping arrangements. Thankfully, the entire upstairs had been cleared out, but to our disgust, it was pretty obvious that cleaning had not been a priority. As we surveyed the splotches, we exchanged a glance of irritation. When we turned on the light in the bedroom, the irritation escalated into full-blown repulsion once we got a look at the decrepit, old, and brown-stained mattress that the sellers had brought up for us to sleep on. Disgusting! What a Gong Show this adventure was starting out as! Having enough wine in our systems to numb the senses and realizing that there really were no other options, we unrolled the sleeping bags, making vows not to let any part of our bodies touch the disgusting mattress, crawled in (fully clothed to ensure extra protection against any biological hazards on that "bed"), and passed out. It would be the one and only night that the mattress we slept on would spend in my home. The next day, it went back to the garage, and would find itself on a trailer heading for the dump in the spring along with many, many other pieces of junk that the sellers had left in the house and around the property.

As it would turn out, I did not form a lasting relationship with the sellers. They had left me with the cleaning of the house, the garage, the shop, and the property—along with a ridiculous home-job wiring of the panel boxes, a terminally leaking skylight over the kitchen island as well as holes in walls, floors and ceilings. There was also a lawnmower that was part of the deal (we would discover that it did not work), a mouse infestation, and many skeletal remains from various animal hunting experiences (which included two small skulls and a bucket of what we think was blood…hair sweater…connection?…eeewwww!) that were scattered around the buildings and yard. Additionally, there was a really nasty confrontation involving the jalopy of that homemade lawnmower from the 1970's they left for us. We would try and try to start the damn thing, but finally we had to haul the pile o' crap off to the dump and buy a mower that worked. I really began to see that I would never like them and, therefore, we would not be forming any sort of friendship. Not long after we bought their property they moved away from the area, which suited me just fine as the mere mention of their names would evoke negative thoughts and bad energy. It was an incredible amount of work to pull this home and the property that it sat on into a condition that was suitable to host the public, and looking back, it was primarily fueled by an enormous surge of anger.

What's the moral of this? Beats me, but it is probably along the lines of, "Like any other sale, don't expect it to go smoothly, hope that the sellers are leaving the area, and, for god's sake don't expect that you won't have naked guests when you take possession of your B&B."

......

Old & New

The sellers were not the original owners, as they had purchased it from the builders who had lived there for many years, according to the info I gathered from our realtor. They built in 1981, so by 2002, when we bought, we knew there would be work coming on the building, which was starting to show its age. We were generally happy with the inspection report, knowing that the only thing that was really on the radar within the next few years was going to be the roof. The home was built full log construction with a cedar-shake roof, a wood-burning forced-air furnace (so you smelled that comforting fireplace-smell outside in all seasons but summer), ten-foot skylights, beautiful hand-carved log-railed porches and staircases, and had very retro-cool hand-painted flowers embedded in Euro-chic designs on door frames and other detail areas throughout. The great room was truly great; 900 square feet with a fifteen-foot vaulted log and shiplap cedar ceiling, it housed the lounging area, dining area, and a large kitchen complete with a ten-foot island with a six-burner built-in Jenn Air cooktop. The guest rooms were furnished with queen-sized beds and had handmade bed skirts, bedspreads, pillow shams, and curtains all made of the same matching fabric offering that oh-so-thoughtfully-finished feeling. Up a private staircase on the opposite end of the building from the guest suites was the owners' suite complete with office, living room, bathroom, and bedroom. There was an attached double garage below the owners' suite and a double detached garage/shop adjacent to the main lodge. The property was four acres that had been largely cleared save a thick perimeter of trees, and it boasted panoramic views of the massive mountains from anywhere you stood. When you drove onto the property on the very large circular driveway you felt like you were transported to a movie set and that this rustic and beautiful alpine retreat couldn't be a real place where real people actually lived.

In the beginning, I often found myself pausing, marveling at how lucky I was; I had the perfect home on the perfect property and I was starting the perfect new life and business with the perfect partner whom I loved, and after so many years together, I looked forward to many more with him in this perfect place. I had no idea that within two years, the perfect business would be shut down for eighteen months while I tried not to drown in a sinkhole of insurance claims and lawsuits (all filed by me and all against others), the perfect home (and everything I had owned) would be just a pile of ashes and charred logs, and that the perfect relationship would then collapse along with the rest of my perfect life.

I had to work REALLY hard to build the business since the client list promised by the sellers never materialized. While TR would work on maintenance and construction issues for a couple of days every couple of weeks (when he made time out from his other businesses out-of-province), I worked on the esthetics, furnishings, licensing, marketing, menus, attended trade shows, networked with other operators in the area, cooked and cleaned for the guests who trickled in, and relentlessly gave every effort I had to build the business.

Two years into my new life things were starting to click; I'm a great entertainer and guests loved coming to "my" place (TR was so rarely there that even a lot of my regular guests never met him and felt, as I did, that I deserved full credit) because I made them feel good with fabulous food and comfy accommodations with all the amenities they wanted, where they could relax and have tons of fun! Summer business was starting to catch on, but my winter clientele was definitely solid after only two years; those who stayed with me would settle for nothing less. I would become friends-for-life with a couple of these early guests who came out four or five times in a season to get their fix of adrenaline rush from their extreme winter sport—snowmobiling. Yes, it was mostly big, strong, testosterony (that's my word and I like it) men in the winters, which I loved because they exuded machismo and saw me as a little damsel in distress (HA!) whom they would protect for the few days they were there. They were also very vulnerable with me; they were hard-working blue-collar boys who had many stressors in their lives—finances, providing for entitled wives and unplanned children, tenuous employment, and yes, many with substance-abuse issues they used to try to fight off all those demons with in their lives away from the sanctuary I provided for them. Using my degree in psychology coupled with my need to be a problem-solver, I was like a therapist who made them gourmet meals and mixed them mean drinks; they were becoming addicted to me and our symbiotic relationship ensured that my winter business was going to be just fine from there on.

Before bed on April 6, 2005, I popped a few logs into the wood furnace and headed up to my space with my beloved and only constant companion, my golden retriever, Hogan (I called him H, like the letter, most of the time). TR, as usual, was not around and by this time the cracks in our ten-year relationship were already showing and, frankly, I preferred H's company by then. It was spring on the property but still winter up in the mountains; that magical time of year where you can ride the snow in the morning and go fishing or play golf in the afternoon. I had one of my "regular" snowmobiling groups arriving the next day and wanted to get a good sleep so I'd have everything done and be bright and cheery for their entrance. I got into my flannel jammies and hopped into bed, then H jumped up and made himself comfy in his fave sprawl at the end of the bed, and away we went to dreamland.

At 4:07 a.m., I awoke to a terrifying and blaring noise. It only took me a second to understand what it was—every fire alarm in the building was going off. In those one or two seconds, I was out of bed and running toward the staircase leading to the great room. I froze solid when I saw, through the ten-foot skylight above the living room, that the roof was on fire and the house was filled with smoke! I ran back to my room and snatched up the cordless phone from its base to call 911. While freaking out with the operator, trying to give her details of my address, I grabbed a duffle bag from the closet and started throwing in clothing, then ripped the underwear and socks drawers open, threw in a few of those, and turned around to head past the bedroom to the bathroom.

I stopped dead in my tracks when I saw my dog still lying on my bed, eyes only slightly open, and he wasn't moving.

In total panic I dropped my bag, bent over the bed, and put my hand on the side of my dog's head. He shifted his droopy eyes to me. I urged him to get up, but he couldn't as he was nearly unconscious from the smoke or carbon dioxide—I have no idea which. I didn't even stop to think about whether I could do it or not; I picked all seventy-six pounds of him up and carried him out of my room, through the upstairs, and headed down the stairs, out the garage door, and into the garage where my truck was. I somehow got the rear passenger door open and laid him on the seat and closed the door to keep as much smoke away from him as possible.

I sprinted back into the main lodge in time to see the first part of the roof breach above the great room and now fire was in the lodge with me. I leapt up the stairs, two or three at a time, and ran to my room. I grabbed the bag and ran into the bathroom to gather a few cosmetics and my valuable jewelry. Tears were pouring out of my eyes from the smoke and emotional chaos by this point and I was sobbing and shaking uncontrollably; I've never been that scared in my life, before or since. The bag was full and it was time to get the hell out of there.

With only those few possessions in the bag, I was running out toward the great room again when all the lights went out; the power-box must have burned up. No lights, no problem—there was so much fire that I could see my way down the stairs, but after going down only a few of them, the roof made a horrible crackle. To my complete horror, most of it then collapsed, burning with epic flames and crashing to the floor within eight feet of my path! Holy shit, I'll never forget that moment; it was when I knew that everything would be destroyed.

I slipped on a pair of boots (I was barefoot to this point) and got out of the house and into the garage. It was really dark in there and I realized that I would have to climb up on top of my truck and open the automatic garage door manually, which I did. It took a bit of time, but in the end, I got out with my dog (who was coming around from his near-death experience), a few personal items, and my truck. I was wearing leopard print flannel pajamas and a pair of big snow boots. As I backed out of the garage, the fire trucks were pulling in and started trying to put out the inferno that was my life. The paramedics checked me over and cleaned my face and hands (I was pretty sooty) while I sat there in shock as an emotional basket-case, at the back of the ambulance, watching almost everything I had ever owned burn to the ground.

In the days, weeks, and months ahead, I would come to really understand what insurance companies were all about, what TR was all about, and how much strength I had. After eighteen months, I would have my B&B back following a lengthy struggle with the insurance company and crooked contractors. After two years, I would have my B&B all to myself as a buyout of TR became imminent when it became very apparent to me (and many others) that he was not someone I wanted anywhere near me or anyone I cared about for the rest of time. After three years, I would list the B&B for sale as I had lost my taste for the entire "dream." After six years, I would be done successfully suing all the crooked contractors and the insurance company. And, after twelve years, I would sell the lodge and move away forever. And ever since leaving, to this day, I keep my houseguests to a bare minimum.

The thing about building new is that you can't build an ageing home that needs updates; it's all NEW and SHINY and MODERN. The "new" lodge was, in a word, awesome. I had a spending limit, so I made some decisions that would enable me to make a bigger lodge with more guest suites for more revenue. The building was still a log structure, but a full two stories with a shocking bright blue metal roof. The great room ceiling was now eighteen feet high, but the skylights were smaller and more numerous. I had log beds made for every room and re-created my fabulous kitchen. Everything was new and beautiful, and I picked every detail of everything that went into that place to ensure that this B&B was going to attract a whole new crowd that would be charged whole new rates.

TR did next to nothing, was almost entirely absent, and had numerous affairs in several of our great Canadian provinces that I would soon become enlightened to. I was then able to manifest the satisfaction of watching him slink away with a pretty lousy buyout thanks to some rather shady secrets about him I threw in his face, which I managed to collect and stash away in a few carefully hidden places. While he was leaving, I was completing the rebuild with the last details of decorating and pristine landscaping including log garden boxes set into an entirely rocked perimeter of the building, a slate/

concrete back patio with a cedar deck and inlaid hot tub. This was all overlooking the perfect garden boxes where I would grow the finest of produce in a painstakingly manicured outdoor display for my guests. There were inlaid flower beds with gorgeous perennials like lilies and the most pristine, thick row of raspberry bushes at the back of the garden area. It was paradise, and I knew it every time I looked at the faces of my arriving guests.

So, you see, there are really two lodges woven into this story, the first co-owned and the second, totally mine. There's the "me" before who was naïve and in love with the boy, the dream, and the guests, and the "me" after who was single, a slave to perfection, and who became cynical but whose drive kept everything working. Then there's the business that, like me, was a bit weak in the first round but came out swinging in the second. The tales you are going to read flow through both the befores and the afters and they are not in chronological order. Instead, I've lumped them into categories of various offences that I endured over the years and have edited many out. Enjoy the ride and please forgive the foul language; some of these stories were written down immediately following the events, so they contain my full and sometimes very colourful reaction.

. . . . .

Here's an email from myself to a group of my friends and family shortly after taking possession of the B&B, back when I believed I was "living the dream"…

Hi all! My life, as you know, has changed a bit. I'm now all settled into life on the acreage of a fabulous Bed and Breakfast in the picturesque mountains of British Columbia. Everything is just awesome and I am loving what I'm doing. It's really quiet here this week due to the lack of snow, (which means no snow-sports) so I have all the time in the world to update you and pursue some of the great country living activities of the area. For example, I spent an hour chasing a fuckin' mouse around and around and around my living room just this afternoon. I saw it first late last night, so this morning (after a really uneasy sleep) I booted it to the hardware store (this has replaced Holt Renfrew as my new favorite shop) to pick up some traps, then ran immediately home to set them and wait for the bone-crushing snap! of success. Not a sign of the little bastard until I was eating my lunch and reading my mail at the breakfast bar, when the monster shot right across the kitchen floor directly from where I had set one of the traps. It shot out of sight, but I thought "that's OK you little shit, yours is-a-coming." My Spidey senses were tingling and I wondered how it eluded the trap it had to have run over, so I went over to check the gizmo and I'll be damned if the trap was still set but the bait was gone! Mad as hell at this point (that hick-chick in the store upsold me to the high-tech and high-priced traps that are "absolutely excellent"), I now wondered how the hell I was going to solve this tiny but revolting problem. I re-baited the trap, deciding to give them a second chance before taking them back to the hardware store and setting them off on her nose... Like in all good horror stories it got dark, very dark, it gets so dark here at night that you can't see your feet. I was lounging and watching a show—satellite TV rocks—when I heard a little squeak followed by my dog growling. Fearless but not-so-smart, he led me to the little prick but just sat there wagging his tail—I think he was amused by the thing. At the speed of sound, I turned on every light in the main hall and grabbed a can to trap the mighty beast and ran back to my dog. I pushed the coffee table over and there it was! I slammed the can down, but the little prick moved fast and ran under the couch; I shoved the couch across the floor and it ran under the other couch; I pushed that couch out of the way and the fucker took off along the wall—right in the direction of another trap. Yeeha! I've got you now! I followed it to the trap behind the CD cabinet and goddammit! it was sitting on the trap eating the bait! Nothing happened! Without thinking, I grabbed a CD and frisbeed it at the trap and Snappo! End of mouse, end of story (except the part where I contentedly picked up the trap—which had half of the thing hanging outside of it—waltzed straight to the guest bathroom, then flushed and released my victim into the "great septic beyond").

Country living is a thing to get used to. It took me years to meet everyone in Edmonton, while it took eight days to meet everyone in the valley. I would never dream of leaving my car or house unlocked in the city, but when I took possession, the owners couldn't find a key to the house for two days because they hadn't used one for nine years. I have to go get my own mail in town at the post office—what the hell is that all about? It's six friggin' kilometers! There's no garbage or *recycling pick-ups, there's a dump, and I don't have to tell you how that's not really an activity that one can wear a suit to! "Later" means "later this week," "tomorrow" means "probably next week," and "yes" is a definite "maybe." I laugh and cry almost every day at my adjustment adventures; after the mouse experience, I have decided that I will do just fine out here and despite a few unpleasantries, I am madly in love with the place and the area. Last week was a continual stream of people and activity, so I've been happy to hit this lull so I can get all my little fixer-upper projects and interior decorating completed. I haven't touched that ridiculous pile of sticks yet—I need months more of cocktails in me before I tackle that little job. It's incredibly beautiful here, I've never seen stars like this before (must be because it's so fuckin' dark!!!), and the locals seem to be as sweet and sincere as I've ever met. I got a booking last night for a family reunion in July from California. There will be sixteen, some inside and the rest wanting to pitch tents and camp for six nights.*

I hope that you all have an excellent Christmas season and I look forward to hearing back from you soon! Take care and Cheers!

· · · · ·

We all go into the B&B business with rose-coloured glasses; our enthusiasm piqued, we are excited to be the best hosts we can be and with optimistic dreams of the "happily ever after." Then reality hits (LOL).

· · · · ·

Chapter 3 - Allergies

A friend of mine has an anaphylactic reaction to peanuts. For those of you who don't know, it means "fatal if not treated right the F now," and because of this friend, I try to keep peanuts tucked out of sight in any home that I've owned. I once found myself calling 911 while jabbing an EpiPen into her thigh as she was gasping for air and turning blue. After a day or so, she was back to normal, but the trauma of the event—the ambulance ride and the several hours in the clinic to follow—will stick with me forever. This is a real allergy with way-too-real reactions, as opposed to all the fake allergies (fads usually accompanied with princess behaviors) I was forced to deal with over the years at the B&B. For the most part, she's pretty good with bringing up her allergy in restaurants, but there have been many occasions where she doesn't ask, so I once quizzed her as to why she didn't "make a big deal about it" everywhere she went. Her reply was that if she's ordering something that never contains peanuts, then there's no point. I disagreed with her, arguing that the pan may have cooked peanuts previously or that there was peanut oil used or whatever! She shrugged it off, so I let it be; after all, it's her problem, right? Incidentally, that 911 call was made from my B&B where she had been looking through the kitchen for a snack and found and ate a cookie containing peanuts that my mom had made and sent to me. My friend expected that cookies in my home would never contain peanuts and therefore they would be safe for her to consume. I should have found a better hiding spot… and you can see that it isn't always just her problem either.

· · · · ·

Why Didn't You Tell Me?!

In my first summer with the B&B, I had a booking from a nice couple from abroad traveling with their two children. When I took the booking, I made the usual inquiry regarding allergies or aversions, and she said that both of her children were celiac. Understanding the gluten allergy, I assured her that I would plan their breakfast to be gluten-free and fabulous, no problemmo!

Prior to their arrival, I went through the usual menu-planning ritual, compiling the ingredients for the black forest ham, Swiss cheese and asparagus crustless frittata, the yoghurt-based fruit dip with fresh cut fruit, and the bacon and potato pancakes. This meant taking ingredients out of the freezer and thawing them, going to town to purchase whatever else I needed (like gluten-free bread), and then doing as much prep as possible so I wouldn't have to get up at 4:00 a.m. to do it all.

I pretty much had everything oven-ready and waiting in the fridge when the guests showed up. After they settled in, the mom asked me about dinner options in town, so I pulled out my menu-brochure collection to show them. They were unhappy with the choices and asked me if I could prepare a dinner for them. As it was already around 5:00 p.m., I had to think of fast things. I could pull out some chicken breasts, then thaw and barbeque them; I had lots of veggies in the garden, so I could grill a few and then make them a killer salad; and I happened to have pears on hand, so I could make some poached pears for dessert. That sounded wonderful to them, so I got in gear and pulled it off to perfection.

The next morning, I brought forth the breakfast once again pulled off to perfection. There was only one problem: "Oh," she said, "I guess I forgot to mention that my husband and one of my daughters have mild allergies to dairy." My gut reaction was to ask her if she didn't think that little detail might be important at a Bed and Breakfast, but instead, as I looked around the table and realized how much dairy was present, I said "No, when I asked you about allergies and aversions you told me about the celiac only." As I stood there with the father scrutinizing me, I felt like a total asshole because of his wife's failure of communication. How unfair is that? I tried to think of something I could quickly pull together for them, but my mind was blank. What the hell do you make for breakfast for someone who is celiac and allergic to dairy? I told them how terribly sorry that I was that I didn't have all the information I needed to make them a breakfast that they would all be able to eat, and I went through every cupboard to try to find something for the non-dairy eaters.

The mom and the one daughter ate like hogs, and thoroughly enjoyed the meal. Unfortunately, I could not say the same for the dad (who was paying the bill) and the other daughter. They had fruit, juice, rice cakes with jam, and black tea; it was the best I could do on zero notice. I received a very "average" review and no tip from this group. I felt like the father thought that I had known and forgotten the allergy info or didn't write it down correctly, but I maintain to this day that his wife didn't tell me. Unfortunately, in doing so, that woman may have damaged my online reputation regardless of the 120% I had put into accommodating the needs outlined in their reservation and the additional efforts put in following their arrival.

. . . . .

I've heard it all on the allergy bit. "I'm allergic to eggs," "I'm allergic to apples," "I'm allergic to coffee," and the list goes on for miles. I always heed the information and will not use the product, as I know exactly what form of drama a really bad allergy can bring. After hearing lists of what you know to be "bullshit allergies," it's easy to scrutinize the dude who very seriously tells you "I'm allergic to anything with 'pepper' in any part of the name, all seasoning peppers, all chili peppers, all peppercorns, all green, red, yellow and purple bell peppers." Doesn't he realize this doesn't sound very scientifically diagnosed? (I didn't think of it at the time but I should have asked him if the list included Dr. Pepper lol.) Or how about the dude who says, "I'm allergic to all vegetables." Yes, he was dead serious, and I knew he was full of crap, and it's a bit shameful for people to call an aversion an allergy. It's not the same, everyone knows it, and they're making themselves lose credibility by using the terminology. OK, I'm done with my allergy rant.

· · · · ·

Pet Allergies

It sucks to be allergic to pets. I know because while I had a lovely golden retriever as a friend and companion for just short of thirteen years, I developed some unpleasant allergic reactions to other people's dogs, but mostly to cats. I have all the typical reactions: varying degrees of puffy, itchy, watery eyes, congestion and sneezing, and itchy skin. As I truly enjoy all of my friends' pets, it never stopped me from playing with them or petting them when I was visiting, but I had to have a general rule of "NO GUEST PETS" at the B&B.

Having been a pet owner for so long, I was familiar, as everyone who travels with pets is, with the pet policies that were in place with so many accommodations. It's the first thing you ask when you book a place, isn't it? "Do you allow dogs?" That is, pretty much, where the conversation starts and stops. And then you get to hear the bump in the rate to accommodate the animal. As a pet owner, you are accustomed to the conversation; and no matter how it finishes, you always feel like you're being bent over a little bit, that you're going to be put in their most horrible space for their most premium rate. It seemed like more and more, it was becoming harder to find an accommodation with a pet that wasn't a total pigsty. At the point of this next story, my dog had moved on to the great dog kennel in the sky so I no longer had to go through that drill. Instead, I found myself on the other end of it, where I had to request an allergen-free room due to the ever-increasing severity of my own allergies.

· · · · ·

How Did You Forget to Mention That?

One spring, I received an email from a company who was coming to the area to do some work on an ecological restoration of a nearby lakebed. There would be enough employees to fill my lodge for five or six weeks, so after some back and forth negotiation with the company's organizer, we agreed on a rate and a price and the terms of the agreement were all set out. She guaranteed the reservation with her credit card and I awaited their arrival, which was to be directly before the May long weekend.

As you would likely suspect, long weekends were busy in a mountain tourism industry, so over the few weeks prior to their arrival I had to deny availability to many inquiries for the time that the eco-company had booked its stay. Because they were staying long-term, I had given them a greatly reduced rate; although I would technically lose money on the long weekend itself, the revenues would be greatly improved by their lengthy visit, so in the end it would work out well for me.

On the Monday prior to the long weekend the first of the crew arrived: three people with three large dogs. I was totally surprised by the dogs, so while the guests waited outside, I politely excused myself to call the organizer and explain to her that due to allergies and cleanliness I did not allow dogs in the B&B. She admitted that she had forgotten to mention the presence of dogs traveling with the group. She explained that they were "outside" dogs, meaning they would be at work with the crews all day. At night, she assured me, it wouldn't be an issue for them to sleep outside—either tied up or in the trucks.

I was horrified by this, as three large dogs would definitely take their toll on my lawn and landscaping, which I spent so many hours manicuring every week. I couldn't sacrifice the first impressions of subsequent guests arriving to a less-than-perfect picture. Because my finances had been drained by the off-season, I reluctantly decided to make the ultimate sacrifice; I spoke to the employees and said that I would designate a portion of the yard for the dogs and that's where they could do their pooping and be kenneled while they were on the property. I told them that they would be entirely responsible for cleaning up after the dogs and also responsible to repair or replace any damage done by them. I thought this was fair; they seemed to understand the problem and also seemed thoroughly annoyed that the "dog" detail had not been mentioned to me. After some deliberation, they informed me that they were not comfortable with the arrangements and did not want their dogs sleeping outside or in trucks, and they left to find alternate accommodations.

Very annoyed, I called the organizer back to report this development, and she had the owner of the company call me. He reassured me that the dogs were fine to sleep in the trucks and that he would arrive the next day and straighten this all out. He said that he would like to stay here but that he, too, had a large dog that would also be sleeping either outside or in the trucks. He assured me that in any event, more employees were coming that would not have dogs, and they would fill the rooms that they had guaranteed me.

The next day, the owner did not show up, but two other employees did with another large dog. I explained the situation to them and the one with the dog told me that he was going to be camping at the work site with his dog, so he would not be staying at my place. The other one, without a dog, said she couldn't stay either because she didn't have a vehicle and would have to stay with the others who would be providing her transportation. They, too, left.

The day before the long weekend, the organizer called to tell me that she had a final three employees who would arrive and be staying at my place the next day (Friday), none of whom had any dogs. I spent the next day at the property doing yard work and waiting for the crew members to show up. They didn't arrive, and I was pissed right off, as now this company had cost me money on the defaulted reservation over the long weekend! And so, I planned a small piece of revenge....

On Saturday, one kid showed up in the late afternoon; apparently, he was one of the three who was supposed to arrive the day before. I took one look at him and thought, "there's no way you are stepping one foot in my beautiful home." He was filthy dirty, disheveled, and seemed to be in a droopy-eyed, stupid-grinned, "floating" haze that I recognized from high-school and early university parties. I'm pretty sure that dude was a connoisseur of cheap weed. I told him to get back in his car and leave my property.

Shortly after this, another vehicle pulled into my driveway. I recognized him from the website; this was the owner of the company. He started interrogating me as to why I had turned his employee away, but I cut him off so fast with one blast after another about his unprofessional actions, his breach of contract, and his overall ridiculous organizational skills that he recoiled with his mouth hanging open. When I finished, all he could manage to come back with was "Yah? Well sometimes shit happens!" Wow, what a loser.

That was the end of that conversation. He got back in his truck and left. I slapped their card with a $600 cancellation fee, which covered approximately 10% of their reservation guarantee. They protested this fee with my card-processing company and there was a lengthy process (like five months) of faxing explanations, journal entries, and other "evidence." In the end, I won the case and the $600, but could have stood to profit much more than that with my regular rates over the long weekend.

What did I learn here? Always assume that the person on the other end of the phone or email has never made an accommodation reservation before, never stayed in any accommodation that wasn't either their parents' house (or crashing at a buddy's), and has never had to think of anyone else's circumstances but their own. Oh, and always be sure to find out if they are allergic to anything even though they won't give a damn if you are.

. . . . .

My Own Allergy Dramas

I'm allergic to dust, mold, and chlorine. How ironic is that? The most effective cleaner and killer of the former two is also on my bad list! The first two give me a terrible time in the spring and summer months, and chlorine makes my skin "crawl" year-round. I spent time and money researching products that did not contain chlorine for cleaning, then endless hours in the cleaning process itself an effort to reduce possibilities of dust and mold. I was so meticulous that I think it actually irritated some of my guests when they saw that cleaning to perfection extended to immaculateness outside also—in landscaping, garden, patios and the hot tub, which gets plenty of attention in this compilation in due time.

The lodge's water source was a deep well. Awesome water except during the spring run-off every year, when there would always be some minor little contamination that would force me to "shock" the system with chlorine. To explain this, when you deal with public accommodations, you are subject to certain government controls like the Health Board (HB). It's a good thing, as they keep everyone protected in some way, shape, or form—but sometimes, I wanted to send them a letter-bomb, like when they'd send me a "disinfect system" notice, usually immediately following a March water sample. I had to send a drinking water sample in monthly to ensure that the water was "safe" for public consumption, which I didn't object to—after all, it provided me with peace of mind as well as relieving me of liability, at least where the water was concerned.

The first time I was told of the "shocking" program was from my plumber who, after I got a notice from the HB, told me that I should do it once each year, regardless of whether or not instructed to by the Health Board. I asked him what, specifically, to do, as he knew my well, cistern, piping, and plumbing—he'd installed most of it. He told me to go and buy ten gallons of bleach and pour it down the well; he said it would circulate into the cistern and then through the system. "Ten gallons?! Are you sure?" He was.

It's important to add that at this time I wasn't yet aware of my allergy to chlorine; I knew the smell made me sick and burned my eyes, and I knew that hot tubs made me itchy, so I never used bleach for anything other than dropping the pucks into the hot tub followed by a thorough hand-washing.

Bewildered, I headed to the store, where I started loading the gallons of bleach into a cart. Just the very thought of how this was going to go made me feel sick and itchy. I couldn't do ten gallons, so I bought eight and dumped in six of them when I got home. Something made me stop there; it could have been the fumes that rendered me temporarily unable to see what I was doing any more.

The next month was closest to the sickest I've ever been; I had a rash so bad that I was scratching until I bled on practically every part of my body, my hair turned brassy and brittle, all of my clothes and linens faded, and I believe that I got permanent damage to my eyes, which have never been the same since that awful time. Shortly after that, I went to an allergist and got the news that I was badly allergic to chlorine/bleach (along with dust, mold, and cats, which I already knew).

In retrospect, I'd made a critical error in that I should have run off a lot of water for several days in a row prior to showering or doing laundry. Not doing so meant that the cistern would only very gradually dilute its chlorine concentration with the gradual replacement of the minimal water I had been using. It was a "note to self" for future, which I wouldn't have to think about again for several years—when I got a phone call from the Health Inspector following my March water sample.

"I'm calling to let you know that there is some background coliform showing up and you need to disinfect your water system."

Me: "What does that mean, background coliform?" I could feel my blood running cold at the thought of the chlorine treatment program.

As he explained to me, it's not nearly as scary as it sounds. It's not E. coli, it's a random contamination, bacterial in nature, not necessarily harmful. After further questioning of this situation, I discovered that it was nine parts per million that we were speaking of, in a sample that may have been isolated, as it wasn't uniformly present throughout even that sample. This seemed a little too random to me, especially given what I would have to endure. I argued this point with him, but he was unrelenting. I explained my allergy and he changed his tune, fully sympathizing with my situation but still adamant that the treatment had to happen. I pleaded with him to find another solution and gave him a graphic description of the hell I had gone through following the last "shock" (what an appropriate name!).

He was appalled by my recounting of the effects I'd suffered. "My god, that's awful! How much bleach did you use?" he asked. I told him and then he moved into his own state of shock. "What?!" he shouted, "Why did you use so much?" I told him that's what I was told to do. "Oh, my god! No wonder you didn't enjoy that treatment! That amount would cripple anyone!" He went on to inform me that with my system, that was ridiculous overkill, and I shouldn't need more than two gallons, but he'd double-check the math with his boss and call me back. He called me back and said, "Glad I caught you before you added two because you will be fine with only adding one." He continued with instructions on how to flush it all out within a couple of days as I listened in my own state of shock.

OMG, how pissed off at the plumber was I at that moment?!

Note to self: If the cure sounds worse than the problem, you had better get a second opinion.

A final pearl of wisdom that can only come from years and years of "living the dream": When it comes to cleaning products, laundry detergents, soaps, shampoos, air fresheners, food (and this one has an endless list of its own!), someone is going to check in who is "allergic" to something you will expose them to. What are you doing to reduce the potential reaction?

· · · · ·

Chapter 4 - There's No Way Your Mom Taught You That

This chapter is all about BAD HABBITS. Everyone has a bad habit, or a vice, or something they do or say that may be simply irritating to others—or, it may be full-on illegal or simply offensive to anyone unfortunate enough to witness it. I smoked cigarettes, on and off, for years. Of course it's not illegal, but it's definitely irritating to others for sure. Not being a total idiot, I understood this and was always very conscientious with the smoking; I would never blow it in people's faces, tick off the ashes wherever, or flick the butts out windows, off people's decks, or randomly out into nature. If there was no ashtray available, I would butt it out on the bottom of my shoe or the road or a rock or something, then put the butt in my pocket to be disposed of in a garbage container later. If you're going to have a shitty habit, at least try not to be a pig about it I say.

I couldn't possibly count the number of cigar and cigarette butts I picked up out of my driveway, yard, and garden over the years. I had ashtrays available outside for smokers, but nothing feels quite as good to some people as flicking that still-lit butt out into a nice gal's beautiful yard once you're done with it. After not too much of this, I got to the point that when guests arrived, one of the things I would tell them is that there are ashtrays on both decks and that's where your butts go, nowhere else, no exceptions. Wow, what a great example of the things you don't think you have to say out loud!

. . . . .

Butt-head

There was a young man who I immediately knew would be a problem smoker as I witnessed him standing less than two feet from the ashtray and flicking his ashes all over my deck. I startled him with an assertive "Hey, use the ashtray!" to which he said, "Oh yah, your house burned down once, I guess you're paranoid." (No, you stupid shit, it's not as much about the fire right now as it is about having a little respect for your hostess and the painstaking efforts she goes to in maintaining her perfectly manicured oasis!) What an idiot. The next night, the idiot was having a smoke in the hot tub with a couple of the other guests. He finished his smoke and flicked the live butt out into my yard, even though the guy beside him in the hot tub was smoking and had the ashtray right between them. I didn't know it at the time because

I wasn't there when it happened, but the good smoker gave the idiot an earful for his disrespectful act. The next day when I was out cleaning and adding chemicals to the hot tub, I saw the butt laying on the snow like a big zit on Barbie's face. When the idiot returned from sledding that day, I took him aside and told him that I had discovered his garbage in my yard, to which he said "I didn't know there was an ashtray there," without apology. I wasn't letting it go just yet, so I said, "Don't bother going to pick it up, I did that for you, as I would have had to eventually anyway." Still no apology, and from what I could tell, no clue that he had done anything wrong. With that, he would be added to the book and the blacklist. One of the good guys that stayed with me later informed me that the idiot had thought that I was a bit of a hard-ass! I guess the smoking rules were too much for him; perhaps one day I'll get the opportunity to dump my garbage on his front lawn.

. . . . .

Stinky and Stalker

Frankly, there is no point to this little story except to expose a few awful habits from two uniquely disgusting men. It's not even a story; it's a description of a couple of totally repellent guys I had to tolerate in my home for a couple of days.

They had been what we all refer to as "high-maintenance" in their booking, even though the dude involved in all communications with me had adamantly insisted that they were totally easygoing and would be happy with all that was provided. He had done a pretty thorough internet search for his group's accommodation, scanning through the various places available and choosing mine as it looked the most comfortable and offered the most complete packages and had the best amenities for their purposes.

As I was saying, the booking process started off easily. In his initial inquiry, he stated that he was coming with four or five guys for four nights. They were new customers, and with the economy being a bit dicey, I told him that I would take the breakfast portion off their bill entirely and have a simple continental breakfast available for them every morning (to include breads, fruit, juice, cold cereals, and coffee/tea) at no charge at all. He was grateful for that, and as we chatted back and forth on email regarding his booking, I got the sense that the price might still be a little too high for them, so in a last-ditch effort to guarantee the booking I offered him an additional $15/person/day off because their booking was for more than four people.

Later, after they had come and gone, I went back and looked through my "sent items" and saw that between his initial contact and their arrival date I had sent him over twenty emails in response to his various questions and "needs," including several that informed me that one by one, his guys had bailed out, and in the end, they were down to only two coming for three nights. Irritating! That's a lot of work to do for a couple of guys who are coming on a very big discount! Of course, I didn't tell him that, but I did tell him that I would have to open up the other rooms for other possible guests as the revenue for that week had now been cut by more than half and expenses still had to be met. As it turned out, it was, by then, such short notice that no other bookings were made, and they ended up with the place and all the amenities all to themselves (which, in retrospect, was far, far more than they deserved and very unfortunate for me, as hour by hour they became creepier and more offensive and insulting than the hour before).

When they arrived, they seemed OK, but it didn't last long. It was after dinner, and they had eaten on the road that night during their travels to my lodge. They walked in and had the usual reaction to the place: "wow," "fantastic," "love log homes." They generally seemed very impressed and were happy with their choice as I showed them around the place and to their rooms to unpack. When they came back, I ran through the "rules" as I do with all new guests regarding the commercial kitchen (you can't go in it), hot tub (it's not a bath tub, you shower or bathe yourself BEFORE you get into it) and my apartment (absolutely out of bounds). They were fine with that, so they had a few drinks since it was too early for bed for them. I thought I'd go to my space and watch a movie, to let them relax without feeling like I was all over them, but they stopped me; they wanted to play a little poker and asked me to join as three is better than two in that game. I thought, "OK, let's get to know you a bit, and maybe I can get a little extra cash out of you while I'm at it!" (I'm no great poker player, but I seem to be lucky and I win way more often than not). So, we sat down, each armed with a drink and ten bucks worth of poker chips; this doesn't seem like much today but at that time you could get a pretty fine bottle of wine for ten bucks!

The usual conversation with new guests began. Guys were always amazed that I was there, in the middle of nowhere, by myself and running a lodge full of men. So, they asked me the usual questions of how I came to be there with the huge house by myself and single (without a man to manage me). My answers were always simple, as I didn't like exposing too much of my personal life. "I purchased this property with my boyfriend, but it didn't work out between us so I ended up buying him out once it became clear that our relationship was ending…No, I'm not rich I had some help from my parents…Yes, it's a lot of work but I enjoy it and there's nothing here that I can't handle; if there's something that I definitely do need help with, I hire someone for the job….No, I'm not really freaked out by having strangers in the house; the years have taught me how to deal with all sorts of crap, besides, you don't know what kind of artillery I may produce if you cross a line (one of my favorite lines; it always made a strong point)….I became quickly alarmed by their forwardness and the inappropriateness of their continual barrage of personal inquiries, which became more and more invasive as the hours and days wore on. "Do you have a boyfriend now?" I always answered yes to that one (whether that was true at the time or not), I'd say that he lived in Kamloops or Prince George and he'd be here in the next few days or something like that. The thing is, a simple notion of an "obstacle" was often enough of a deterrent to ward off advances or other inappropriate behaviors. I soon learned that these guys would be deterred by nothing. Stalker immediately wanted to know how often we got to see each other and how often I was "getting laid," which began his nickname in my mind, and it would only become more appropriately chosen as time passed. Stinky voiced his opinion that we were probably "banging the shit out of each other" every time we saw each other. Remember now, I had only just met these swine! In all fairness to the rules of equal exposure, they were quick to volunteer all sorts of what I would think would be private details of their lives, and without my asking. However, their activities in the bedroom didn't interest me, and I was starting to get really, REALLY creeped out by these two.

Over the course of their stay, Stalker said the following things to me: "Boy, you need a good F-ing," "Your boyfriend must love F-ing you," and, my personal favorite, "You're bad, you need a good licking," with a seething, skin-crawling grin on his face. Disgusting, gross, yuck! His semi-good looks were negated by his repelling demeanor. He was a big boy too, well over six feet, big and solid and likely strong enough to be a real problem, so I can't even express how uncomfortable he made me and how I was counting the seconds before he would be out of my life forever. At some point, he made conversation by telling me about a Bed & Breakfast that he and his wife once stayed in. Apparently, the owner was uncomfortable with the noises that were coming from their bedroom. This idiot told me that the owner made him so uncomfortable that he and his "old lady" (love that term, it reeks of class!!!) couldn't have sex. If I were to take a guess at what actually went down, I would have to say something more along the line of "he was banging the shit out of her and the variety of noise that it created raised a few eyebrows at breakfast the next day."

The poker game itself was horribly unpleasant, as this is how I came to "Stinky's" naming. Stinky was, well, stinky. Hard on the nose with all the great sound effects that his flabby body could produce. He had uncontrollable farts that he enjoyed tremendously. It was like he was trying for a better, louder, longer, nastier one every time, and they were very frequent. He claimed to have a form of colitis which caused this side effect, but he was simply a bit of a pig, as he made no effort to leave the room or even offer an apologetic "excuse me" when they shook the room.

I don't remember another thing about them or their stay at my place, only that they offended my nose, my ears, and my intellect profoundly with their incredibly disgusting bad habits.

· · · · ·

The Drop-Ins

Dropping in, in my opinion, is unacceptable. I don't drop in on anyone, ever; I have always called first to make sure that it's a suitable time to pop in for whatever reason I'm making the visit. This is normal, as most people I talk to share the feeling that dropping in unexpectedly is a bit disrespectful and usually a total imposition.

I know you're thinking "you own a B&B, you should expect drop-in customers," and you're right. Oddly, they were few and far between, and when they did drop in on me unannounced, I tried my best to be a gracious host and not to look annoyed by their lack of a reservation or consideration. These days, most people make reservations in advance as they have a manifesto to stick to. The only ones that don't are the "free spirits" who go where the weather takes them that day, and they are usually low-maintenance, fun, and friendly folks to host. I rarely had any trouble from drop-in-B&B-strangers; they were almost always guaranteed to add a pleasant element to the week.

The paying guests are not who I'm talking about here; I'm talking about friends and acquaintances—these, by far, are the worst offenders. For some strange reason, it's the people that we know who seem to disrespect our time and space the most by not bothering to let us know that they are going to descend on us. If you asked me to, I couldn't count the number of times that I had to inform my acquaintances that "you should have called first."

I would get home from a game of golf or a grocery run or any little outing to find a note on the door, or later receive an email or text saying something along the lines of "Dropped in to visit (or "looking for a bed," or whatever) but you're not here!" It always sounded a little on the accusatory side, like they were a bit miffed by me not sitting there waiting for them even though they didn't bother to let me know that they might be coming. "Dude, you should have called first! If I know you're coming, I'll be home; if I don't, I might not be around." Or, I'd get a phone call out of the blue, "Hey, I dropped in on you last month, but you weren't there. Did you go on holidays?" To which I'd reply, "Nope, I've been here all summer, but I usually go to the gym then play golf, so I was probably out. Try calling first next time (Jackass!)." It was hard to bite my tongue, when I felt like saying "Do you really think I'm sitting here waiting on the million to one chance that you're going to pull into the driveway today?" The crazy thing was that they knew my number and had been in their cars driving for at least five hours and it didn't occur to them to let me know they were coming to my house. Even if they had given me only one hour's notice it would have been cool; whenever I left the lodge, I call-forwarded the phone line to my cell phone, so they would have found me. But that never seemed to occur to people; they'd drop in and then be surprised, inconvenienced, and irritated if I wasn't there.

Then there were the "friends" who would drop in and find me at home. This would go one of two ways: awesome surprise, or imposition, inconvenience and irritation to me. It was in the vicinity of a 50/50 split. Some of the excellent surprise drop-ins included my Godparents, my previous cocktails-every-weekend neighbors from our family's lake property, and various other close friends from my past lives. Although it was awesome to see them and I was glad they stopped by, I was still a little confused as to why they didn't bother to let me know they had been coming. I always made a point of sliding in a little comment like "Next time call before you come so I don't miss your visit." Sometimes it sunk in and sometimes it didn't. And then there were those surprise drop ins by "friends" that caused nothing but imposition and annoyance....

· · · · ·

Losing Patience with The Chronic Dropper-Inner

Before I moved to the lodge, I lived in a real city, had a real job that I got because I had a real education, and lived a real city life. When I left my job, I kept in touch with very few (less than a handful) of my colleagues, as most of them never became close friends.

Within a year of my moving to the property, a work acquaintance showed up at my place one day. I didn't know him well; I'd known him only from the business and the associated social events but never hung out with him in my personal time. I'm pretty sure he was halfway drunk already when he arrived, and because I hadn't been up to anything much, I invited him in. He came in with a bottle of rum that was coincidentally around half full. Over the next couple of hours, he drank the other half and passed out on my couch.

Before I got up the next morning, he had started in on another bottle of rum and was in no condition to carry on with his journey. I tried to convince him not to drink all day and to eat something, blah, blah, but he was having none of it. He wanted to get drunk and pass out again, and that's exactly what he did. I shook my head at the whole thing; WTF kind of BS is this? But there's no point in trying to make a point with someone who's loaded; we all know this is a huge waste of time.

I didn't get a chance to give him any opinion on the matter, or a bill, as he was gone the next morning before I got up. That pissed me right off—not even an offer to pay for his two nights' stay or the small amount of food that I had convinced him to eat. He didn't even leave behind a token gratuity for my inconvenience!

I didn't hear from him for a long time and then he started phoning me, horribly depressed as everything in his life had gone to crap and he was usually drunk and not making a lot of sense in the calls. I didn't have the heart to lay more misery on him with my anger at his taking advantage of my location, as he was so down and calling me because he needed someone to talk to. I felt even sorrier for him that there was nobody closer to him than me, an acquaintance from work from several years before. Over the next two years, he dropped in by phone several times, and then the calls stopped.

Close to a year after the calls ended, on a cold day in February, I was doing mid-week room turnovers between guests when there was a knock on the door. I opened it and there he was, grinning and looking much more together than I had seen him since I had left the city. I was genuinely happy for him; I don't want to see anyone in a toxic state of being and I had a little time, so I was looking forward to hearing how the transformation had taken place. In greeting him, I put my arms out for a hug, but he said he had to pee so bad that the hug would have to wait until he used the washroom. "Sure, right down the hall," I directed as I laughed at his childishness.

His shoes were off and he was running down the hall as I turned back to close the front door. I paused as I noticed that his truck was still running and the voice in my head was nothing short of pissed right off. OMG, he dropped in only to pee; I was reduced to a urinal on the side of the highway! I turned the voice off and tried to tell myself that nobody would be that brazen, but the voice was right. He came out of the bathroom still grinning and went right back toward the front door to slip back into his shoes. "I can't stay and chat—I have to get to the city to see my folks, but next time for sure I'll stop and chat." I was so shocked that I didn't even know what to say except, "You came here just to take a piss?" He said, "I'm really sorry but I've got to go!" as he ran out the door, hopped into his truck, and took off. Holy shit, I thought my head was going to explode I was so mad! He would never step foot in my door again.

He must have realized that this incident was nothing short of rude as I didn't see or hear from him for almost a year and a half. How could he not realize it? I can't imagine showing up on someone's doorstep only to use the bathroom! This is exactly the reason that rest stops are all along the highways, and there was one less than 500 meters from my driveway, and he'd traveled that highway enough times to know it was right there!

Fast forward that year and a half, and it's the middle of summer and I was getting ready to go to a dinner with a couple of friends in town. The anger that he had caused me was nowhere near my thoughts on this hot, sunny summer afternoon. I had put on "girly" clothes and jewelry, and was slipping on a nice pair of summer sandals to show of my pretty pedicure when I glanced out a front facing window. His truck was stopped on my driveway, out toward the highway and my mood instantly went black like a hailstorm. As I glared at the situation, I deduced that he must be having drama with his truck as he got out and moved to look under the hood. "Oh, no you don't," I said to myself "you are not going to use my property as your mechanical stop either." I grabbed my purse, locked the door, pulled my vehicle out of the garage, and hit the button to shut the auto-overhead door. In my rearview mirror, I saw him walking toward my house.

I didn't shut off my car when I pulled up to where he was. I opened the window, and he stood there grinning again and was about to say something when I angrily said, "I'm just leaving." He said, "There's something weird going on with my truck…" but I cut him off, saying, "I'm not a mechanic; I can't help you. There are several mechanics in town; take your truck there if you need truck help and while there, you can use their bathroom. I'm sick of you dropping in without any notice like this is your personal rest stop. You've always had my phone number and have not once used it to let me know you were coming. You drop in with no regard and no respect for me or my time. No more! Now you deal with your own drama because it's not my problem!" He tried to plea, saying, "I'm sorry! I don't have your number in my truck!" but I wasn't having any of it. "I have to go; your truck is blocking my driveway."

It must have been obvious to him that I was mad and not going to relent, because he turned and started walking back to his truck while muttering something inaudible to me. I stood there solidly holding my position as I watched him drive away—and not in the direction of the mechanic's (the problem couldn't have been that pressing)—thinking to myself "Yah? F-you too." He had finally been cured of his bad habit; he never called or dropped in again.

· · · · ·

A Scary Dropper-Inner

On a gloomy and snowy/rainy March day in my ninth winter season at the lodge, I was immersed in a "me" week as I had a cancellation in the schedule. I had been enjoying a productive few days of completing projects that had been shoved aside, eating nothing but fish, seafood, fruit and veggies (this was an unacceptable diet for the regular clientele who would surely perish without meat and potatoes at least twice/day), and incorporating at least two and a half hours of exercise or workout into every day to get the tone and freshness back into my form.

On this particular weekday, the weather was particularly bleak, the highway passing the front of my property particularly quiet, and I was in my second-floor suite absorbed in yoga. It was warm inside, so I was wearing only athletic shorts and a tank top; I was barefoot, wearing no make-up, and my hair was twisted up in a loose knot on top of my head. Clearly, I was expecting no one to show up at my door.

In the middle of a yoga stretching-pose, my heart stopped cold as I heard someone loudly turning the front doorknob back and forth trying to get in. Let me be clear here; they did not knock, they were trying to get in. Instant terror overcame me as I realized my vulnerable situation, dressed in not much more than underwear and very much alone at my acreage in the middle of nowhere! In a split second, I snuck over to peek out of the window to get a look at the vehicle to determine whether I knew who it was, but there was no vehicle in the driveway! The person was still trying to turn the doorknob, so in the other half of the split second, I grabbed the cordless phone and moved over toward the upper landing to peek down into the great room and out my front window so I might be able to see who was on the deck near the front door. I peeked around the corner just in time to see a man peeking in my front window! He did not see me, as he did not look up to the second-floor landing. Before he could look up, I ducked out of view and moved back toward the window where I would be able to see him leave (I was really hoping that would be soon, otherwise I would have to make a 911-call before my nerves completely shattered!).

It seemed like minutes, but it was only seconds before I saw him step off my front deck, quickly walk down the sidewalk to the driveway, and with an unusually brisk step continue all the way out of my property to the north, on foot to the highway. Then, he crossed the highway, and in a half jog, half walk, he came past my property going south on the far side of the highway until he was out of sight.

I will never know what he was doing; who was this random person running through my property, trying to get into my house then running away down the highway? I called a friend and she was as perplexed by it as I was; who on earth would not knock and opt instead for trying to open the door? After much debate, we decided that it must have been a motorist whose vehicle had crapped out somewhere down the highway and they were on foot trying to get help. Any other possible explanation made my stomach turn over and gave me heartburn.

Needless to say, I had a really shitty sleep that night.

. . . . .

Years and years of being dropped in on left me looking over my shoulder all the time. I began to look out the window toward the driveway all the time to see if someone was coming to surprise me. If I was coming into the great room with the giant picture window, I would do so by looking around the corner and peeking at the driveway first before committing my whole body to full view by someone who may have been pulling in. When I was upstairs and I heard a car pull in, I would survey the situation between the blinds before deciding if this was a welcome visitor or not, and then either answer the door or pretend I wasn't home. I stopped suntanning in my bikini in the backyard. I stopped leaving my truck outside the garage so there would not be any sign of me being home. I never left any doors unlocked, and I would do all of my personal hanging-out, like watching TV, napping, or reading, upstairs, in my second-floor suite with the blinds shut where nobody could see me if they pulled in. It was, seriously, the only way that I felt like I could control what was coming in and out of my life.

It's depressing to live like this; in a constant state of paranoia that someone is going to intrude and wreck your day. Unfortunately, when you own an accommodation business, this is what you can come to expect; your freedoms and your privacy are forever redefined.

. . . . .

Manners, anyone?

I was not raised to be pretentious or condescending. I was not reared to be a princess even though I remember my mother telling me to "Try to behave as if the Queen were here." I am grateful to my parents who instilled the value of being well-mannered in me as I now know how to behave in any number of situations and always with appropriate manners for the venue and the company.

Sadly, I was visited by a lot of people who seem to have been raised by swine. As usual, all names have been changed to protect the ignorant (God knows why, these Cro-Magnons don't deserve protection).

A particular guest must be referred to first. It was like watching a car accident in slow motion: you don't want to see what's going to happen next, yet you can't help but stare.

Mike came up with his wife, Janet, for a winter getaway on sleds. She was great; outgoing, funny, a gracious guest who I enjoyed chewing the fat with in the mornings and evenings. Mike, on the other hand, was quiet and pretty shy—he often seemed not to even be a part of the conversation, drawn off into his own little world. Very inconsistent with his reserved personality were his appalling manners.

Have you heard someone "hoark" before? That's my dad's word for when you suck up the goop in the back of your nose and throat and then hairball it up through your mouth and blast it out of your lips with a huge nasty cannon-ball throat-oyster. It is possibly one of the most disgusting acts to do and should only be executed in extremely private circumstances, not at the F-ing breakfast bar! Yes, I got to see this every morning at least twice; what a great way to start your day, thinking about someone else's snot! His snot-capades didn't end there, either.

A gal I worked with had once enlightened me to the phenomenon of "blowing snot." I was horrified to hear that there are primate-men out there who plug up one nostril with a finger and blow like hell to shoot the snot out of their other nostril (she's from Saskatchewan, for the record). This is, apparently, considered to be an "outside" activity for the most part. Mike was the guy who demonstrated this grossness for me for the first time in my life. I was shocked and disgusted by this. I did not care that it was outside, as it was on my property and I would inevitably step in it at some point in the spring thaw. I was so grossed out that I called up a good friend of mine in Jasper to report the incident. She was not at all shocked to hear of the act. "Oh yeah, a snot rocket," she said. Apparently, there are a few primate-men in Jasper, too.

. . . . .

I had another guest who insisted on waiting to say anything until her mouth was full. Not so hot. Then, she would hold up a few fingers to her mouth to try to cover up the fact that she had horrible eating manners. People, if there's food in your mouth, do not talk! Chew and swallow and THEN move to conversation. You want to go visit their parents and slap them for making you deal with the crap that was their responsibility to dial back.

. . . . .

Lip smacking has always pissed me off. It pissed my mom off (my dad does it a lot!) and you quickly learned not to do it in her presence. My dad comes from a long line of lip-smackers; he had a tough time breaking the habit, but after years of tongue-lashings, mom got him to rein it in a bit. I am surprised at how many people smack their lips while eating. The thing about it is that there are two elements of gross at work here: 1- The sound makes your flesh crawl; and 2- To smack your lips, the mouth must be open so everyone gets a good look at the progression of the chewing of the stuff in your mouth. This is not something I need to watch, ever.

· · · · ·

Knife-licking, plate-licking, horribly offensive and sexist comments, burping, and yes, farting are very much a real thing that the public brings into your home no matter how beautiful it is, so you had better be prepared to witness, smell, hear, and tolerate of them. It's normal for some people and they wouldn't dream of altering their behavior for any reason, even if that reason is to appear less piggish to a stranger than they actually are.

· · · · ·

Help Yourself! It's a Bed & Breakfast and Anything Else You Feel Entitled to...

My mom was a master at growing heirloom tomatoes. She had a buddy who seeded enormous amounts of them annually, and he used to give her so many each year that mom and dad's place looked like a tomato grow-op some years. Of her collection of seedling plants, she would give me a selection of different sizes, shapes, and colours to nurture to growth each spring, as I had the giant acreage and the space in pots and gardens to host the plants. I cherished them and took better care of them than I did myself most days. I would check the forecast two or three times per day looking for signs of hail or other destructive forces so that I could run to their rescue and move the potted ones to shelter, and I always had a system in place to cover the ones that are permanently in the garden. I could never afford to build the greenhouse (with a deadbolt) that would suit the extreme beauty and craftsmanship of the B&B, so I had to settle on log raised beds for my pampered veggies and tomato plants. This meant that all of my beloved vegetables were out in the open where they were vulnerable to any of nature's beasts that may decide to take an interest in them. In retrospect, I rarely had trouble with members of the animal kingdom where the coveted garden was concerned.

One year, mom gave me the usual batch of a dozen or so of her different seedlings, two of which produced cherry-types of fruit, which were expected to grow very tall. I carefully picked out a large pot for each of those two that matched the housed perfectly, planted one cherry-type in each and placed one on either side of the front steps, where they would get afternoon sun and also benefit from the heat of the house during the cool mountain nights. They were amazing producers; early in the spring I could see that each plant was going to have at least eighty little gems for me to savor throughout the summer. Anyone who has grown a tomato plant knows that the best fruits are the ones that are left on the vine to the moment of consumption, so I always left them to turn that brilliant and mouthwatering red before twisting them from their lifeline to be enjoyed within hours (or seconds!).

By June, the first ones began to turn red. Strangely, as two or three would be two days away from "perfect," they would disappear. This happened again and again, and at first, I thought a scavenger from the forest was coming for treats during the night, so I didn't react, thinking that the little thief probably needed them more than I did. As June moved into July and I still had not sampled my elusive gems, I started noticing that, coincidentally, the tomatoes were disappearing every time I had guests. Time after time, I'd look at those two plants and notice the just-about-ready tomatoes vanish from the vines with the arrival of the next guests.

It's important to mention that not one guest asked me if they might have one; it was as though they assumed that they were fair game for help-yourself. With this realization, I felt a bit violated that guests in my home would take my tomatoes without asking. Upon cluing into this phenomenon, I gave up my credo of vine-ripening and as part of my guests' pre-arrival checklist, I picked all the orange tomatoes from the plants and let them ripen in a bowl in my OFF-LIMITS kitchen window. That year, incidentally, it wasn't until August that I was able to enjoy one of my own tomatoes, but I'm pretty sure I saved the vast majority of the remainder of them from the unentitled bandits.

It always amazed me that the guests felt that my tomatoes were included in the rate. So, apparently, were the raspberries, peas, zucchini, carrots, and anything else they decided to pluck from my garden.

Another thing you don't think you have to say: PEOPLE, THE SIGN DOES NOT SAY "BED AND BREAKFAST AND U-PICK"!!!

. . . . .

Wedding Guests from Hell

Ah, weddings! An excuse, for many, to get loser-drunk. You know what I mean? This next one is an accounting of one that will forever be burned into my mind; here's another email sent to my friends and fam:

Hey, y'all,
I had seven guests of a wedding staying here; they were guests of the bride's parents who live in the area and made the booking with me. The arrangement had been that they were getting a substantial discount on the rate because the bride's parents, I thought, were sort of friends of mine and asked for a break in the price for these guests. This wedding ended the practice of giving discounts to "friends" and also ended whatever form of friendship had existed between me and the parents of the bride.
The guests arrived two at a time and the seventh was last. Upon arrival everyone

seemed pretty normal, definitely from lesser-education backgrounds which was apparent in their language, grammar and social graces, but pleasant enough not to raise any serious red flags at that time. Upon arriving they all had wedding stuff to help with off my property, so they disappeared to do that, came back in the later evening and went to bed; they all made some comments about getting a good sleep for the huge party the next night.

The day of the wedding most of them got up and took off to go help with more prep before coming back to the house in the early afternoon to get ready for the main event, which included pounding in a stupid amount of alcohol while sharing stories that were so ridiculously offside I had to make a conscious effort to close my gaping mouth about a dozen times. Finally, they left for the wedding and I was in great relief because I wouldn't have to listen to the low-class banter anymore. Little did I know it was going to get much worse. Here's an email I sent to a couple of friends outlining the events that occurred over the night, accompanied by a picture of them sporting their Walmart wedding-wear. I couldn't make this up—these are real guests staying here this weekend.

From left to right:

(First Couple's Names): *After a couple of wobbly pops he likes to ask EVERYONE to sleep with him. I wonder what his success rate is????? She must have an extremely high tolerance level.*

(Female2): *Obviously has had a rough ride and doesn't mind sharing those stories with strangers.*

(Male2): *A bit of a chameleon; he seemed classy but then blended well.*

(Female3): *Age fifty-four and still working the spandex. Nightwear: yellow string bikini, two sizes too small for the enormous bust line.*

(Female4): *Female 3's daughter. A three dressed up as a nine and believes that (real quote from before the reception and still sober) "I don't have to pay for drinks, I have tits."*

(Female5): *I'm not kidding, that's her name (it's a name only a SUPER-hillbilly trailer-trash could have). Note that she smiles with her lips together to avoid exposing that very much absent tooth in the front of her mouth.*

This morning there is an eighth person, female, snoring loudly on the couch in the living room. I have no idea who she is and it's possible that she doesn't either.

The last group got back here from the reception at 4:30 this morning. They thought it was TOTALLY unreasonable that I asked them to be quiet twice after their arrival out of respect for people sleeping both in this place and on neighboring properties. (You know how when you've over-indulged sometimes you think that every one around you is hearing-impaired and so you compensate by using your "football stadium" voice and also that every little syllable from anyone's lips is the FUNNIEST thing you ever heard, worthy of your shriek-laugh?) The father of the bride was with them and stayed for more drinks with a few of them until about eight this morning, when one of the others FINISHED THEIR (twentieth?) DRINK AND DROVE HIM HOME. One of the last things he did before he left my property was drop his fly and pee on my lawn.

It's settled; I'm writing a book.

Pretty harsh, eh? There are many details missing, but you can fill in the blank spots; however, that's not where it ended. Here's the email update sent out a few hours later after they had removed their disgusting selves from my lovely home:

Update: The couch-sleeper is the mother of the bride, actually a very nice person and totally horrified by her husband's actions; she'll probably take a round out of her hubby later when she finds him. "Toothy" brought home a local kid for a good time; I just got a good look at him and I've decided that steam cleaning in that room will happen before the next guests arrive.

Wedding Dress: 8 bucks, secondhand
Drinks: nothin', 'cause I got tits
The fact that nobody's embarrassed: priceless.
For everyone else, there's MasterCard.
Take care, talk to you soon,
S.

Unbelievable! This is how the public acts in your home. There was a final act that was not emailed out and is being relayed here for your enjoyment.

After checking out, Male2 called and left a message that he had lost the keys to his truck. When I listened to the message, I laughed my ass off at that! I searched his room and found a hairbrush and a pair of dirty socks but no keys. He stated in the message that he was coming by to see if I had found his keys, so I put the items I'd found in a plastic bag to be given to him on his arrival.

When he arrived, I was upstairs and saw him pull in. He got out of the borrowed truck, but rather that move toward the house, he leaned up against the vehicle and pulled a joint (this was long before the legalization of weed) out of his shirt pocket and proceeded to smoke it in my driveway. Now, I ask you: Who the F does that?! I could not believe it and it pissed me off that this idiot thought that this was an acceptable behavior.

I grabbed the bag, walked out of the house, and handed it to him. Without hesitation, I turned around, came back inside, and shut the door—just as he tried to ask if I had searched everywhere. Had I checked under the bed? Was I sure they weren't hanging on the hooks on the wall in the room? I didn't answer anything; I said, "They're not here, buh-bye now." From inside the house, I could see him standing there, looking stupid (and pretty stoned) for a while, and then he got in the truck and pulled out.

I never did receive the apology from the father of the bride that was promised to me by his wife, so you can imagine that I don't care that our "friendship" became non-existent as of that day.

· · · · ·

Chapter 5 - Damage

It's inevitable that from time to time a guest will damage something in your home. It's rarely an "accident" in the true sense of the word. Accidents are unplanned, unfortunate events that happen by chance and with no intent. You think of an accident as an unavoidable happening that could only have been a product of fate or a higher power than we ourselves possess. Thinking back on the accidents that happened in my house and the damage that was caused, none of them could be defined in these terms, as they were all a product of too much booze resulting in stupid behavior that caused damage to my stuff.

Yes, sadly, your things are at risk. Nobody cherishes them more than you do, so hide the breakables and be prepared to enforce a repair/replacement policy, because the only thing more inevitable than the damage is the guest's unwillingness to take responsibility for it and then to make it right again.

. . . . .

The Lamp

My favorite lamp was given to me by my grandmother when she moved from her home into an assisted living facility for seniors. She and my grandfather had purchased it new in the 1950s in Southern Alberta. It's teak and looks a little like a tree: big brass floor base, six-foot rounded centre with five teak-with-brass accent arms that extend outward in various directions. At the end of each arm is a large glass tulip-shaped housing for a lightbulb in bright red, blue, or yellow.

When TR and I purchased the B&B, I had decided to put the lamp in the main part of the lodge, the great room, up against a wall and out of harm's way, or so I thought.

It must have been either the first or second year that we owned the B&B that TR brought out a group of guys that he knew from somewhere in his suspicious travels. This wasn't unusual, TR brought out guys from time to time, but it really got to the point that I wished he didn't bother.

TR had strange expectations for the accommodations for his pals. Here's an interesting one: The first time he brought out friends, he told me that I should not give them a bill. That's right, he expected me to house and clean up after this bunch, feed all of them three meals each day, and then not bill them. What the F?! I couldn't believe what I was hearing and questioned his request. He explained that they would leave a large tip instead. I didn't like this at all, having been in the hospitality industry for most of my life I knew there were many people out there whose idea of a large tip wouldn't cover the toilet paper that they used. I put my foot down and told him to forget it, and he came back with "When your friends come to stay you don't charge them, so you can't charge my friends either." You can guess where this went, can't you? "Well, TR, when my friends come here, I clean up after them and I do all the cooking. They always leave behind a REALLY large tip and generally help with the clean-up. Since this time they're your friends, how about I take off for a few days and you do all the cooking and then ALL of the clean-up including the bathrooms, laundry, and floors, and then you can keep the tip. When I come back it must be ready for the paying reservation due to arrive at the end of this week." I'd be surprised if he could make toast or do laundry, so this was obviously not an acceptable arrangement. The argument continued, and in the end, I agreed to try it his way. As it turned out, he won that battle but not the war as their "tips" were as insulting as their obnoxious, rude, sexist cavorting. After this experience, like all the other "guests," they received a bill from me every time they came back. As a denouement, in our fourth year of ownership, exactly as the way the billing of his friends went, we agreed to disagree on everything that we shared, and I bought him out. Both our personal and business involvements with each other were dissolved and I would never host him or his friends again.

With that little bit of background into my former boyfriend and business partner, I can now get on with the story of the lamp.

A group of TR's friends arrived and they were as unimpressive as they could try to be. Out of shape, sweaty, unattractive, horrible grammar accentuated by their incredibly foul language, and generally without any manners whatsoever. I couldn't believe that they wouldn't tone it down a bit once they realized this was a hard-working female's home. Who knows, maybe it was toned down!

To make a long story short, they got drunk and the lamp was broken when one of them couldn't keep his balance. His eyes wandering and arms flailing, he stumbled his eats-too-much-crap frame backward into it and crashed it to the ground. When I heard the crash, I rushed into that room to see what had happened and saw him lying there stuck on his fat back, dazed and trying to get up; he looked like a beached whale on top of my beloved lamp.

Once the drunken pig was declared unscathed, he was removed from the crash scene and my focus turned to the lamp. One of the brightly coloured tulips had been smashed. I picked up the pieces and cleaned up the mess.

I was pissed right off and told TR that his friend would be responsible for the replacement of the glass tulip. TR thought that I was being ridiculous. He said that I should expect things to get broken sometimes and accept that as part of the wear and tear on the place. I agreed that may be true for things like glasses or plates, but when someone gets so inebriated that they can't stand up, then stagger into a valuable antique and break it, the incident can hardly be described as basic wear and tear. I told TR that I would look the lamp up on eBay and on antique auction websites to find a value, and then I would add that value to the disgusting boor's bill. AND THEN THE FIGHT WAS ON, as the saying goes. TR was not going to let me bill the fat prick for his damage, and I was not going to let this incident go unpunished or without compensation.

In the end, TR and I came to a compromise. He took the broken tulip and one of the tulips that was intact to a glassblower who made a replacement tulip. His drunken loser-friend was not invoiced for it; it was TR who actually covered the bill. From the few comments that I received from TR, it was an expensive, time-consuming, and irritating chore, but I thought that's the very least it should be for he who had the "jewels" to suggest that I should smile off the incident entirely.

Once repaired, the lamp went back to its place in the great room where it stayed until one horrible night when the entire lodge was consumed by flames and I lost almost everything that I had ever owned. Remarkably, amongst a few other coveted antiques, the lamp went with my father on a restoration retreat. My dad had taken courses and knew what to do, and when I moved into my newly rebuilt lodge (TR was bought out during the rebuild), the lamp was returned to me in mint condition.

· · · · ·

The Lamp, Part 2

Once in its new home, my beautifully restored lamp sat in its place in the brand-new great room where I was able to enjoy it daily for about two and a half years.

I didn't normally take guests over Christmas, as it was too weird to have other people do their Christmas thing in my home. Not really a "Christmas" person, I would either spend that time alone, as everyone else generally had plans, or go to a friend's place. Over this particular Christmas, I had no bookings for either Christmas or New Year's and no plans to leave my home. I invited my friend to come out for a New Year's dinner as she didn't have any plans either.

It was one of those rare occasions where I had a date coming also, so my friend asked if she could bring one of her employees who I didn't know at all. He had only been working for her for a short time (I wondered if there was something going on between them) but she enjoyed his company, knew he'd be alone for the evening, and thought it would be a nice gesture. Because I understood that being the third wheel was always a bit of a drag, I welcomed this even though having a stranger in my home for New Year's was a little bit awkward.

And so, everyone arrived: my date, my friend, and her employee, who turned out to be twenty years younger than me and with whom I would find nothing in common. My date was a particular breed of social gregariousness; he was tall, dark, and handsome, and loved to be in the centre of attention, exuding confidence and humour with his big voice and striking presence. He knew my friend and talked freely and openly with her and took every measure to include her employee in conversations and make him feel welcome in every way. Because they were both male, I also think that helped to aid in easing communications. We ate a celebratory dinner, opened "special occasion" wines, and spent the evening having a relaxed mini-party.

Very unfortunately, there was a little too much alcohol consumed. My date and I were having a little dance in the kitchen while my friend and her employee were having what looked like one of those country dances where the couples are whirling around the dance floor with incredible momentum and skill. The only difference was that the dancers in my living room had too much booze and not enough skill. They crashed into my beloved lamp and sent it to the floor, breaking two of the tulips this time. I could feel my blood boiling.

We cleaned up the mess and I took the unbroken part of the lamp upstairs into my private living room where it would never be subject to public abuse again. I tried not to let the incident mar the rest of the evening by simply stating that they would pack up one of the unbroken tulips, take it with them, and find someone to replicate two more to replace the ones they broke. I didn't want to talk about it, didn't want the apologies to go on and on, I just wanted the damage fixed. They agreed and took the pieces with them when they left the next day, promising to have it done as soon as possible.

I'm writing this story eleven months after that incident. As far as I know, there were steps taken to replace the tulips and restore the lamp, but as time passed it may have slipped into the back of everyone's minds (obviously everyone's except mine). As I sit at my desk, I have the lamp directly in front of me on the other side of the room. It's been standing there ever since that night it was last broken. It's not as beautiful as it once was, as it is still missing three of the five glass tulips that have yet to be replaced to restore it, once again, to its mint condition.

My beautiful lamp was finally restored twenty-two months after its damage and would never leave my private suite again. Folks, save yourselves a world of disappointment and hide the valuables!

. . . . .

The People Stew

Hot tubs are disgusting. If you want some great advice, do yourself a favor and post a "no food and no glass" rule. You should also post somewhere that it is closed at a certain time and then you lock it, as you don't want to wake up with a floater in your pool because he was "overserved," decided it was a good time to jump in the hot tub, and then fell asleep and drowned.

Prior to owning the B&B, I had a hot tub at my home that was treated with bromine. I, like many private-use hot tub owners, chose bromine because of its gentleness on the skin. I've always had sensitive skin, so that choice was a no-brainer. When I bought the B&B, I discovered that public-use hot tubs must be treated with chlorine, as it is far more effective as a sanitizer (bug killer). This was long before the introduction of saltwater tubs, so at the time it was the only option. I soon had to stop using the hot tub myself, as it turned out I developed a terrible allergy to chlorine. Had I not developed this allergy, I would have stopped using it anyway as I became thoroughly appalled and disgusted by what the public does to them.

Any idea how a ham and pineapple pizza looks the next day in a hot tub? Gross. Hot tub closed for three days of cleaning and flushing of filters and lines.

What do you think of a stupid, drunk man who cannonballs in wearing flannel pajamas? Hot tub closed for three days while new filters are ordered and installed.

How about another drunk who drops his drink on the side and the chunks of broken glass fall into the tub? Then the idiot decides that rather than get out and tell me, he and his idiot friends will continue tubbing until one of them slices his foot open on one of the glass shards, and gushes blood all over the inside before he decides to get out and look for a bit of first aid! Hot tub closed for a week, more flushing, more filters ordered, and serious germicidal cleaning due to the blood.

I bet you don't think anyone's going to have sex in there—this is your home, after all... HA! I had the auspicious gift of accidentally walking in on that one more often than I will ever admit.

I bet you don't think anyone's going to pee in there! HA! I've seen three to four dudes drink a few cases of beer, and nobody gets out the whole time.

I've walked outside and surprised guests (and surprised me too!) who decided to have a who-can-pee-the-farthest contest from inside the hot tub. Because there was snow on the ground, they couldn't see that the garden was exactly where they were peeing to. I told them that the vegetables that I served with their dinners were all grown in that garden, so I hoped they enjoyed the fact that they had eaten their own or someone else's urine from last year with their dinner. Then I told them to grow up and NEVER do that again.

Guests always ask me if they should take a shower before using the hot tub, and I always answer, "Well, should the guy before you have?" Another great answer for the guy who came back from a day of outdoor exertion is "It's a hot tub, not a bath tub, so use your head and get the "swass" off yourself before you dip yourself in the hot tub I have to clean later" (for those of you who don't know what "swass" is, check it out in the Urban Dictionary online, LOL).

Females, surprisingly, are the worst offenders, as they most often will not shower before and they enter with all the deodorant, body butters and lotions, perfumes, and whatever else they have applied to their skin since their last shower. You can always tell when a girl has been in because the water gets a grey-brown, cloudy colour. Minimum three hours of attention and scraping the caulk from her body off the sides of the tub. No, it does not get sucked away into the filters; it's oil-based, especially once it's mixed with your body oils, so it congeals in disgusting blobs to the walls where it builds up and remains until you clean.

Tans are brutal. Tanned skin is dead skin, and dead skin falls off. Where does it go? The answer, sadly, is not "away." Its conclusion is exactly the same as the girl basted in body butter.

Cigarette butts and bottle caps are a commonly occurring yet rarely explained phenomenon in hot tubs.

Oh, and one last thing. The longer people sit in the hot tub, the more of themselves get left in there for you to scrape off at a later time.

Gross.

· · · · ·

Chapter 6 - Why Are You Not at a Hotel?

People are going to do strange things in your home, and you will ask yourself over and over again, "Why would these people book a B&B instead of a hotel room where they can act any way they want to and nobody will see it?" You will be perpetually shocked by their "vacation-brain" thinking (or lack of it) and the behaviors and situations that come from it. You will never cease to be amazed by the things you will see, smell, hear, have to touch, and hopefully, never have to taste!

. . . . .

High-Maintenance Living

One day during the summer, I had a couple from Alberta arrive. An interesting anomaly with Albertans is that they have no idea what time it is. Everyone else IN THE WORLD knows that the portion of the planet containing most of British Columbia is in what's called the "Pacific Time Zone" and it's one hour earlier than the next time zone moving east, the "Mountain Time Zone", that contains the whole province of Alberta. In mathematical terms, this is how you do it: "N" (the time on your watch in Alberta) - 1 = Pacific time (time in BC). When you're on the highway and you cross the border from Alberta into BC, there's even a big sign stating the time zone change and that you should move your watch back by one hour. It's not complicated, yet the Albertans seem to have a tough time figuring it out.

The couple from Alberta had been told, as they all are, that check-in was 4:00-9:00 p.m., as they saw on my website when they made the booking. They showed up at 2:30 p.m., and I was still doing the day-to-day yard work, although I had fit in my workout and shower earlier, so at least those important items were out of the way. When the noticeably overfed couple got out of their car, I greeted them and commented, "You made it here in very good time; you're quite a bit earlier than I expected you." He looked at his big, shiny Albertan watch and in his big, booming Albertan voice said, "Well, only half an hour," to which I replied, "Dorothy, you're not in Kansas anymore." With a light-hearted and obviously forgiving giggle, I added in my syrupy-sweetest voice, "In BC, it's one hour earlier than Alberta." Things you don't think you have to ask people: Are you sure that you know what time it is? They both had a big laugh over that but didn't even ask me if I was prepared for them at that point;

they were already grabbing their things and moving in for their stay.

I took them in and they marveled at the sensational great room, as almost everyone did, upon entering the building. He quickly regained his composure and threw out something like "These log homes are great, and so easy to build I don't know why there aren't more of 'em around." There was no point in even entertaining that conversation as he, clearly, had no idea what he was talking about and was too dumb to realize the insult he had just given me. Instead, I gave him the look of "you've got to be kidding!" You know the one: one raised eyebrow and same side of mouth in a half-smile-half-smirk. She let out a nervous chuckle and covered for him with "It's just so beautiful, it's even better than the website makes it look!" while I was leading them to their room.

At this point, I need to mention that with the preparation of each room, the number of towels and bathrobes (with logos—very nice!) were placed within to correspond to the number of guests to be in that room. Each room was colour-coded; the towels and robes were deep, rich, luxurious colours, and they were of the thick, high-quality terry that you would expect in the better hotels. In the bathrooms were the same colour-coded washcloths and hand towels. By the door leading to the hot tub was a stack of hot tub towels that were of less quality and, therefore, of less consequence when colour-damaged by the intensity of the chlorine necessary to maintain sanitation of the hot tub, or as I liked to call it, "the people stew" (aka "dude soup," LOL).

As part of their settle-in, the Albertans wanted to freshen up. They both took ridiculously long showers, each of them running the water for a minimum of half an hour. It irritated me knowing that this was wasteful behavior, but I bit my tongue and continued on as the gracious hostess. They looked cute in their bathrobes; the size M she wore and the size XL he sported barely covered their overindulged bodies, but the looks on their faces of complete pampered bliss made me take a little pride in my provisions and forgive their environmentally unfriendly showers.

Once the freshen-up period was through, it was time for them to have a beer or two. As it was a perfect summer day (around 25C and totally windless) I thought they might enjoy themselves more on one of the decks (one in the sun or the other in the shade for those not wanting to get nailed with UVs), watching the birds and enjoying the fabulous mountain views. No, they preferred indoors, as they didn't want to get sweaty before going out for a nice dinner; I had to mentally admit to myself that they looked like the types who could likely work up a sweat by merely drinking a beer. They asked me for ideas on where to eat and so, because they were all dressed up and stated that they wanted to have a "nice" dinner out while on vacation, I recommended the restaurant in town that would be considered the "highest end" of all available in town. I showed them all the menus that I had, and they perused every one and agreed that the restaurant I had recommended was the best choice for what they were looking for.

Once they left for dinner, I picked up the empty bottles they left on the coffee table for me to deal with and cleared them into the recycling station, and went into the bathroom and hung the wet towels they had left on the foot-ends of my hand-crafted log beds up on the towel hooks that were on the walls. I then hung their robes (one on the floor, one on a bed) on hangers in their closet. I went into the bathroom and wrung out both the washcloths that were sopping wet and lying in the bottom of the tub and hung them on the towel rack, picked up the bathmat (also sopping wet and rumpled on the floor), and hung it over the edge of the tub. Nice.

When they returned, they came inside and opened another beer each. I asked them how their dinner was, and they said it was OK, but I could tell by their manner it was more like "not good". I asked them what they had ordered, and they answered, "Well, we weren't really hungry so we just ordered burgers." Red flag! They don't serve burgers at that restaurant! They changed the plan! "Where did you eat?" I asked them, to which they responded again that they weren't really hungry so they had decided on burgers and fries (if you're not "really" hungry you're going to shove in a big fat burger with a pile of greasy fries?). On top of this, they went to the restaurant I specifically told them NOT to go to because although it's big food for the cheapest dollar, it's also not good, and they were dressed for a much better venue. It turns out that "cheapest" was probably the only word I needed to use, and I shouldn't have bothered with the recommendation process at all. So, they had a few beers to drown their sorrows before changing and grabbing the tub towels for a trip to the hot tub and then another long shower each (much to my surprise!) before turning in for bed.

I was up early the next morning, as usual. I was making them an unforgettably delicious menu of Mexican persuasion and carrying out every detail to perfection. Even though I generally had no warming to this couple, I always like people to go away in amazement of the food, particularly after coming off a disappointing dinner as they had the night before. We had pre-arranged the time for breakfast to allow them to sleep in and then have a leisurely meal al fresco, on the back patio in the warm morning sun, but shaded by the big umbrella over the table.

They rose with enough time to squeeze in one more half-hour shower each before breakfast was served. By this point, I was completely mortified by their water abuse, but made a vow to myself to hold my tongue as they would be gone soon and my well would have a chance to recover from its recent overload of work. I served their masterpieces and came back in the standard three-to-five-minute period to see how everything was and if there was anything else that they might need to enjoy the rest of their breakfast. They raved about the food, how wonderful and unique it was, and how much they were enjoying me, my beautiful home, and my fabulous breakfast. Then they invited me to join them while they dined. Normally I don't accept this invitation because I have learned that people's table manners are atrocious and I don't ever need to see the food-maceration process through its oral entirety while being told something that usually ends up irritating me for the rest of the day. This time I accepted, poured a coffee, and sat down with them to ask them one important question.

"How is it that you found and chose my place for your stay?" "Oh!" she gushed, "We ONLY stay in Bed & Breakfasts; we love the comfort, the food is always delicious, and it really suits our lifestyle!" I could plainly see their capacity to voraciously devour indulgent and fabulous food, but I didn't get this last point and felt like asking them if she should rephrase it to "our piggish and embarrassingly consumptive lifestyle." She then went on to tell me that during the night, she had woken up because she had to go to the bathroom. When she came back to her room, she decided that rather than risk waking up her husband by getting into the bed they were sharing, she got into the other bed to sleep for the next three or four hours. I had a hard time keeping a straight face through that little piece of "info-sharing." I kept thinking that every owner of every B&B they ever stayed in was going to ask themselves "what the hell are these people doing here? They are motel-people like nobody else I've ever witnessed!" We continued with small talk, and after breakfast they each spent another period of time in the bathroom (lots of flushing and tap-water running), paid their bill without tipping me even five bucks, all the while spilling forth what a wonderful time they had and how perfect everything had been, and then they left.

I then went about my business of stripping the bedroom and bathroom and preparing for laundry. One couple, one night and six way-too-long showers later, here's the whopping three-extra-large-loads of laundry list:

> 4 bath towels (that's right, they went into another room and got two more when I wasn't looking)
> 2 hot tub towels
> 4 wash cloths
> 2 hand towels
> 2 sets of bedding
> 2 bathrobes

The next day, the bathrobes were removed for the summer; if guests were here for only one night, they did NOT need that luxury. In addition, I removed the hot tub towels, on suggestion of a friend I'd called up to rant about this experience. She suggested that the guests get one towel each and they could use it in the hot tub. When the towels became noticeably bleached, I could donate them to the SPCA and get new ones; this made good sense to me! The final renovation inspired by this couple was that the following signs were created and put up in each of the bathrooms and remained there until I sold the joint and moved far, far away:

PLEASE CONSERVE WATER

Water is one of our most important natural resources, and it requires everyone's efforts to protect the supply. Please consider that you can:
- Hang your wet towels for reuse during your stay
- Keep showers short
- Avoid running excess water at all times

FYI, they took the toothpaste too.

· · · · ·

High-Maintenance #2

Another tale of people who are DEFINITELY not the BNB-type:

I had a couple arrive from New Jersey; they had booked through Airbnb for five nights. That's a long time if things don't go well, so it's a good idea to get a feel for them before they arrive so you can (hopefully) anticipate and avoid problems. I had been communicating with them through the website to ask about dietary concerns or allergies (nope, none!), offering them advice on hiking, attractions, and other things going on in the extremely popular summer tourism market. He was grateful and loved the tips, thanked me, and asked more questions on all the hiking they wanted to do, which I happily answered. This kept on until a few days before they arrived; it seemed like they were excited and energetic about coming to the area and to my B&B.

When they arrived, I was a bit surprised by their appearance; these "hikers" were both VERY overweight, looked like they were struggling to get up my front step, and were a bit short of breath from the forty-foot walk from the car. I could not help but wonder how they planned to do all this hiking that he had planned for them. I showed them around and gave them the usual "welcome" speech, but was interrupted by him asking me info on the hot tub he saw on the website. I him that gave him the usual disclaimer line that it's not a commercial tub, so technically guests aren't allowed to use it, but that I didn't mind if they decided to, provided they were out by 11:00 p.m. ("quiet time") and that they used the hot tub towels (yes, these made a necessary come-back) over by the door. He immediately challenged me, stating that "We can use it later than that; we're very quiet." I was a bit shocked by this and told him that no, they would not be allowed to use it later than that, as this is my rule, period. Then she butted in, "Do we have to wear bathing suits?" OMG, really? To which I responded, "This is my home; I am moving around in it, sometimes inside and sometimes outside, and you might be as uncomfortable having me see you naked as I would be having that surprise."

I then had to change the subject to avoid thinking about their hot-tubbing rituals any longer. From our previous web-chats, I knew that they would likely be spending one day doing not much and "hanging out" at my place, so I asked him which day was going to be this day of rest as I had contractors waiting to come do work and a showing of the lodge to a potential buyer. He would not commit to a day, and turned it on me to ask if that was going to be a problem. I immediately told him of course not, but I'm a busy girl during the day, that's why the place looks so great—so as long as you can amuse yourselves, that's golden. (BTW, this is the standard response for people who want to hang around all day. I don't care, but I'm not your entertainment; the deal is bed and breakfast and nothing outside of that.)

I went back to the welcome speech that was interrupted by their nudity BS and finished up with a couple of points including "no smoking inside, but there are ashtrays on both decks, so please use them." Again, a challenge from him, "I like to take a walk around to smoke," which scared me a bit, having lived through a "complete loss house fire". I told him that was not going to be possible given that, "It's dry season and the forest fire danger rating is at HIGH so please keep the smoking to either the deck or the graveled areas around the house". I already disliked this dude—I mean, is he for real? Walking into MY house and telling ME how it's going to be? Kind of dickish, yes?! At any rate, as it turned out he wasn't a cigarette smoker, he was a pot smoker, which was why he wanted to wander away; I found this out the next day during a conversation that he led into weed. Glad we got that cleared up, but once more I was dealing with a pot smoker, which was unfortunate because they're all the same: entitled. "Pot should be legal; it's totally harmless and everyone knows it's going to be legalized soon, so I'm just going to smoke my pot and pretend that it's legal and that everyone else is an idiot." This is more or less how they think and this was the basic speech I heard from him over and over through the next five long days.

The next morning, they emerged for breakfast as I was plating it, at exactly the time they had requested it the night before. I cheerily greeted them and wished them a good morning and offered coffee/tee and ushered them to the table where all was laid out: grilled quesadillas stuffed with scrambled eggs, bacon, chives, cheese served with hash browns, homemade fresh salsa and an orange-slice with fresh raspberries garnish. Also on the table: avocado slices, sour cream, two kinds of juices, and the usuals: salt, pepper, ketchup. Here's how he began the conversation me, "Wow, this looks great, but I don't really eat tomatoes." Nice time to let me know that little tidbit. So, I asked him why he didn't let me know that when I asked him a month ago. He responded that he didn't think tomato would be on the menu. Then, before he ate every little bit of food on his plate except the fresh salsa, he covered everything on his plate with ketchup. Before they left for the day, he made a point of telling me that he was surprised that with my commercial licensing I would have regular appliances, and that he expected much bigger equipment in my kitchen. As the days slowly ground on, I learned that neither one of them knew how to cook at all, so it irritated me even more that he would pretend to know a thing about kitchen appliances and that he would have the nerve to kind of toss a bit of a dig at mine.

The next day, the breakfast menu was fresh blueberry pancakes with slices of fresh strawberries, dollops of Greek yoghurt and fresh raspberry jam with maple sausages, and fried eggs. As I placed their plates in front of them, she looked at the food then back up at me and informed me that she didn't eat any meat that was "ground". OK, maybe the tomato (that didn't squirt from a bottle) was something they may not normally expect on a morning plate, but sausages? Really? Is this a foreign concept for breakfast in New Jersey? I wanted to rip on her for keeping that from me, but again, I said, "Hey, when your hostess asks you for your dietary concerns, you should be honest." It turns out it wasn't that big of a deal, as he ate all of her sausages with lots of ketchup. On the remaining mornings they informed me that they didn't eat bell peppers, fruits with skin, or asparagus, all of which had just been put on their plates of food.

I can't remember if it was the first or second morning that I asked them how the bed was, as I always asked. I'd always hear rave reviews, but his response was, "Well, I'm just being honest, but the bed is not good, it's too soft and it has a big dip in the middle." I was stunned as I had NEVER had a complaint on the uber expensive beds. The problem was that they were both so overweight that they were sinking into the middle and squishing each other, so one of them got out of the bed and slept in the other bed in that room. I was sympathetic to their problem and offered them an opportunity to try another bed in another room, I considered that the bed that they started in might be getting worn out so a mattress that had seen a little less traffic would work better. They took me up on that offer and tried one, and then they went back to their original room after an hour or so because that one was "just as bad." It's a point to note that no other subsequent guest had that complaint regarding the beds.

Here's how the "down day" went: got up for breakfast and then she went back to bed until 4:30 p.m.—not kidding, 4:30 p.m.! Who does that?! When she dragged her sizable caboose out of the "saggy" bed and blessed me with her presence, she complained because she didn't get much sleep during the day because the contractors were at my place working on the satellite dish replacement. He hung around most of the day and did things on his laptop; he didn't seem to enjoy the day at all, and I think he was irritated by the contractor activity also and by the fact that his girlfriend was being a bit of a Debbie-downer. Then they went out for dinner, and when they came back, they complained about the food they had and then made themselves peanut butter and jam sandwiches for a second dessert.

They honestly seemed like they didn't enjoy anything about my beautiful house, the beautiful area, or their beautiful holidays through the Canadian Rockies. I was so glad to see them leave because their energy had been so negative that I felt like I wanted to close the business and go get any other job. Then there was the clean-up and the laundry count for two people, five days:

    3 full sets of bed linens
    5 hand towels
    5 face cloths
    4 hot-tub towels
    6 brand-new cream-coloured bath towels, 2 of which they had badly stained with blood

On their way out, he tipped me $80.00; I supposed that it was either for appliance upgrade or new towels.

·····

Chapter 7 - The Assholes

I'm sure you're thinking, "Wow, I thought we were already made aware of at least a few of the assholes!" You, my friend, are quite wrong. The folks you've encountered so far didn't qualify for this chapter as they were all more to be pitied than scorned (an expression borrowed from a friend; LOVE it!). They are likely the product of their own environments and can't help the fact that they were raised without ethical values or lacking training in consideration and good moral conduct.

This chapter and the next address the jackasses that seem like they are actually making the effort to be nothing but shitty. This special breed of folks think that they are very smart (and you will discover they are the opposite!) and that the rest of us will not see through their lies and their subsequent excuses when they get "caught" in a lie… or while engaging in a totally unacceptable act. They will never "own" their behavior, and they don't admit being wrong or even attempt to offer an apology because they are just the right combination of arrogance and stupidity to think that they are right even when all other rules of society, and sometimes even the laws of our country, are telling them different. You'll see what I mean - let's get on with it.

. . . . .

The Double-Booker

I had a booking from Edmonton for four or five guys from a customer that was what we'd call a regular. I would see him around four times in a season, but usually in very small groups of two or three. This particular group contained mostly new guys who had communicated to the booker that they had checked out my website (which had all the rates posted) and were looking forward to the stay.

You need to understand a bit about the guy who made the bookings. Thinking back, he usually traveled in small groups likely because he didn't have a lot of friends who wanted to live in close quarters with him for days at a time. He was a real snob, but I could never figure out why. He didn't come from big money or royal bloodlines, he didn't have an extensive secondary education, and he didn't work in a field that was at all glamorous. He had worked as a blue-collar tradesman for most of his adult life after getting a ticket to operate a particular type of machinery and married a gal whose dad owned a company that was able to parlay his training into a career that was very well paid. He had "retired" from the physical career and moved to teaching his trade. Good, honest work but nothing high-profile or with many letters following his name.

This dude was not the typical tradesman: he was meticulous in his personal grooming, designer-focused in his wardrobe, and his "toys" had to be nothing but the best of the best. He had good grammar and a decent vocabulary and when he spoke it was with confidence, wit, and seemingly strong knowledge, but you could tell he was a lot less clever than he thought he was. He was a bragger; he loved to tell you tales from his life that were "expensive": vacations, cars and other toys, expansive home renovations, blah, blah. His personality could be described as immature; a control freak who pouted if he didn't get his way or wasn't the centre of attention at all times. He had a pretentious attitude that made it seem like he thought he was above everyone and treated most people with condescension; he never even used his wife's real name, but would refer to her only as "Dearest," which I always found a little offensively misogynistic. He demonstrated a general disrespect for women; on a previous trip, he made a particularly offensive comment that I should hire hot, young girls to put on and take off the tarp on his sled before and after his rides. He thought they could be the "tarp tarts," and he also thought he should bring this up again and again even though he saw my obvious disgust on the first round. He would complain about anything he could come up with and would never hesitate to point out if others were doing something that he didn't agree with; but, most importantly, he was NEVER wrong. I can't count the number of times I thought "You're so wrong, you have no idea how far off base you are at this moment," but I soon learned not to bother with any correction, as it was guaranteed to be wasted on him. As you can tell, I never cared for him.

Because the other one or two guys that he usually traveled with were pretty good guys, there was never any damage or disrespect to my home, and it was a reliable revenue source for my business, I could smile my way through his crap for a few days here and there. There were many occasions to wink or roll the eyes with his pals at his expense during his stay, which made up for one or two of his irritating comments while he was around.

Around ten days before their slated arrival, he called to cancel the booking because most of his group couldn't come so they would have to reschedule for another time. I was disappointed but not angry; these things happen and that's that; you can't hold it against them. I understood and we ended the conversation on a pleasant note. After the call, I was thinking that the crappiest thing was that I had turned away other bookings for that weekend and knew that it was unlikely that I would get more as most people make their reservations at least a couple of weeks in advance. The best I could hope for would be a couple of guys on a last-minute booking. As it turned out, my intuition was right, and I ended up with no guests that week.

The phone rang on the day the group had been scheduled to arrive, and it was the most entertaining snowmobile guide in the universe on the line. Lemons were going to turn themselves into lemonade. When he asked me if I could come out sledding for a couple of days because he wanted someone to "tail" the group he was guiding and take pictures for them, I jumped at the chance since I had nothing else to do and loved to get out and play in the snow whenever I could. We made the plan for hooking up the next day, which would start out by meeting his customers at the parking lot of one of the sled areas for the standard safety talk and avalanche equipment training.

The day turned out to be fabulous. Fresh snow, blue skies, the always-amusing guide, and three excellent guys from Saskatchewan who were mesmerized by the beauty and terrain of their first mountain-sledding experience. You couldn't put together a more perfect day if you tried, and I mean it, they were great guys and we all had a great time sledding through the virgin powder at altitudes surpassing the tree line all day.

At the end of the day, they invited the guide and me to come back to the lodge they were staying at for a couple of wobbly pops, and we happily accepted as it was on the way back to town anyway. When we arrived at the lodge, we met the new managers, a husband-and-wife team, who, it would turn out, became good friends to me. We instantly "clicked" and happy hour, like the previous part of the day, immediately turned into a great time too.

The boys grouped together to talk about rpms, four-stroke innovations, diamond-drive reverse systems; all the crap I had to listen to every day and had learned to block out way before, while the wife (let's call her Rose) and I chatted about the area, the odd little town, the accommodation business and its customers. The lodge they ran was close to twice the size of mine and could house at least double the number of guests, so I was curious to know if they had any other guests this weekend to fill this great big place. Yes, they did; there were four or five guys from Edmonton who had arrived the night before and would be there for exactly the same amount of time that my cancelled group had booked. They would be back any minute, as the daylight was fading, and they were having their dinner, as with all of their meals, at Rose and her hubby's lodge that evening.

As you can guess, my "Spidey-senses" were tingling. I could not resist the temptation; I narrowed my eyes, grinned a sly grin, and in a low and very suspecting voice, I asked Rose, "What are their names?" Yep, it was him, the little prick that had made the booking then cancelled on me, telling me that it was because nobody in his group could make it. To make matters even worse, the group he was there with was the same group of guys that he had booked with me. I told Rose the story and we did a quick date comparison and realized that the dude had booked both places himself. He had booked their place before he had cancelled mine; the asshole had double-booked and then lied to me on top of it.

Rose, like me, enjoys a bit of controversy, so we agreed on what a nasty little act had been performed and wondered if he should be taught a little lesson. We quietly told her hubby what was going on and asked his opinion. Dan (hubby's fake name) was annoyed that the little runt had pulled this and said that he didn't like the dude at all as he had been snotty, demanding, and a general prick since he'd arrived. He was on his venting trip when the guide stepped up to the bar and wondered what Dan was going off about, and without any hesitation, Dan spilled it out. The guide shook his head in disgust at the story, but then started laughing loudly when he realized he was going to have a front row seat for the look on their faces when they walked through the door and saw me sitting there having a cocktail with their hosts.

The guests that we had guided had overheard part of the conversation and wanted to hear the story too, and after a bit of persuasion we let them in on the drama that was unfolding. As other booking customers, they were also pissed off by the lying and double-booking practice and made comments relating to how that's clearly wrong and you shouldn't do that, especially in a tiny little community where the odds of getting caught are high. Everyone agreed that I should stay until they arrived so the double-booking liar would know that he was, indeed, caught. I'm a little embarrassed to admit that we were all enjoying the anticipation of the confrontation ahead.

It wasn't much later that we saw the group pull in and park. As it happened, they knew before they shut their trucks off that I was inside because I had driven that day and so parked right next to them was my sled (as well as the guide's) on my trailer being pulled by my truck. It was an unmistakable trifecta and there wasn't anyone in my sledding customer base that wouldn't have recognized it.

They solemnly lingered in their trucks for a long, long time while we watched in the warmth of the crackling fire inside the lodge, savoring our libations and laughing our asses off at them. When they emerged, they didn't come inside. They checked every gage, belt, light, plug, brake, track, tunnel, body, throttle, blah, blah on every sled they had. It was so funny! You will never see such blatant procrastination as we witnessed that day. The guide laughed the hardest, as he had about the most experience and expertise with sleds and sledding as anyone I had ever met, and he COULD NOT BELIEVE the extent to which they were coming up with things to check instead of coming inside.

At last, one of the guys in the group (that I truthfully liked) started to make a sheepish walk toward the lodge. When he walked in the front door, he weakly smiled and said hello to all of us. He looked right at me with no surprise on his face. He looked very uncomfortable, and I detected notes of regret and a bit of guilt. I felt a bit sorry for him and sensed that he had found out exactly what his buddy had done and realized that he may be held guilty by association. He wasn't the one I had the big beef with; I was pissed off at the one who double-booked and then lied to me about the cancellation, and so I tried to communicate a message of peace by pleasantly smiling at him and offering him a friendly "hi" back.

He beelined around the chalet, getting a drink, hanging up wet gear, going into the dining hall, and ending up face-to-face with me near the bar. "We were supposed to stay at your place, but a couple of the guys were too cheap to pay that price so we ended up here." "That's not the story I was told, I was told the trip had been cancelled altogether and that none of you could make it," I replied to him. What could he say? He knew I would have no reason to make up that story so he apologized for the cancellation and the obvious irritation the actions had caused me. I told him that he didn't need to apologize; he wasn't the one who did the double-booking and then told me a big fat lie to get out of it. I assured him that I had no beef with him over this incident, but I was careful not to mention that the other guy was in one heap of kaka as far as I was concerned. That was pretty much the end of our conversation, and he went back outside to continue helping the other guys out with the tinkering. I, and everyone else, immediately knew that he had been sent inside to "test the waters." It's like throwing a hat inside a door to see if the dog inside is friendly or tears it to bits with its fierce teeth and claws.

While their group was still all outside, the inside group came to an interesting revelation. I'm not sure how we ended up on this track, but at some point, it occurred to the managers of the lodge that they thought the double-booker was pulling a fast one on his buddies also. They explained that when he made the booking, he gave specific instructions that he would pay the entire tab and that the other guys would pay him their shares after the trip. This was not so strange; lots of guests work their groups this way. The managers said that what was more than a little bit strange was that he had added that he did not want anyone else in his group to even get a look at the bill. It was something that he had repeatedly reminded them of, the last time being the day before, when they had checked in. It was all to be billed to only him, and he did NOT want the rates discussed with the members of his group at any time. Then he said something about himself being a guide and adding a guiding fee along with gas and other expenses. Now the "other expenses" are understandable, but the "guiding" part had the red flags popping up everywhere.

"Guiding," in BC, means that you are commercially operating a recreational business on Crown land. In order to do this, you need government approval in the form of what's known as tenure. To get tenure, you need to submit your business plan and registered business information plus your commercial liability insurance policy (that will usually cost you many thousands of dollars) with a cheque for the tenure fee to the Lands Branch, and then you may or may not be approved for your guiding operations. It's a drawn-out procedure that costs a great deal of time, effort, and money, and every step must be carried out to the letter.

As the double-booker had no recreational business licensing to begin with, there was no possibility that he possessed the tenure necessary to be a guide and, therefore, no legal right to charge a guiding fee. We all had a hunch that he had used my rates to charge his group the accommodation fees and then added on an illegal guiding fee after relocating the group to a less expensive (nearing half the price per person) accommodation, without communicating the rate change to his traveling partners. Pretty tricky, eh?

If we were right, there was no way he was going to get away with it.

After a while, most of the group came into the lodge. The double-booker lingered outside alone while the others settled in for a drink and introductions to me and the real guide and the other guests. The real guide steered the conversation toward guiding, and casually slipped in a few informative comments regarding his guiding certifications, insurance policies, and other guiding criteria as the double-booker's guests listened with narrowed eyes of growing suspicion.

The double-booker's guests grew a little silent, so my new friends, the lodge managers, then opened up a new conversation around how they were planning to raise their rates, which had remained unchanged for several years. As we casually discussed the rising price of Hydro, food, and other expenses of a lodge, the guests listened intently. When Rose stated that my prices were practically double theirs, the guests looked like they had been stun-gunned. They immediately asked her what her rates were, and when she told them they exchanged angry and knowing glances among themselves but held their tongues.

One of them was so pissed off, he stomped out of the room. When he returned, he had composed himself and calmly told the managers that he would like to have a copy of the bill when they left. My new friends happily agreed, and we knew that our hunches had been correct and that our work was now done.

The real guide and I thought it was time to head out. The lodge guests would be having dinner soon and I didn't feel like I could add any more "insult" to the proverbial "injuries" that the double-booker's guests would have in store for him. As we said our goodbyes, made a plan for the next day's trip, and gathered our gear, the double-booker came into the lodge. He offered me a guilty looking "Hello" and said something like how at the last minute they had all been able to go. I gave him a good long stare, communicating with my eyes that I thought he was full of crap. I offered him a dismissive "Whatever" as we walked past him and out of the lodge. I suspect that he was dragged through the dirt over the next day or two and that his "guiding" career was about to end, along with a friendship or two.

A week or so later, the double-booker called me at my lodge from his home in Edmonton. Caller ID is great; screening calls rocks, and this was one I definitely wanted to take. It went just like you might guess; he continued to try to feed me the BS and I let him know that I didn't think very highly of his lies. It ended with him blurting out that he could stay anywhere that he wanted to and to this I pleasantly replied, "You're right, you can. You can stay anywhere you want to from now on except here." I hung up and I never heard from him again.

· · · · ·

The Most Dysfunctional Family on Earth

I had a "family" book into the B&B for a week one year. There was a dad with his three sons aged thirteen, fifteen, and seventeen. The last guest on the roster was the one who made the booking and all arrangements for the group, the father's younger friend, business partner, and, as I would find out later, a roommate and alternate "father figure" to the family. The ex-wife of the older "dad" and mother of the children came up in passing only once in a conversation, and so I casually asked about her the next day while they were hanging out at the lodge. They all got noticeably uncomfortable and quickly changed the subject, and she was not mentioned again during their stay. Not a big deal—there's no rule that states you have to disclose past relationships, especially the ones that seemed to cause so much discomfort. It was a bit of a red flag and a little sad to me, as I value my own relationship with both of my parents, who have always been and will always be together and function as the "glue" of the family.

But I'm getting ahead of myself. This story has a definite and amusing beginning, so I'm going to get back to it so you can savor the magic of this appalling group from start to finish.

A few days before the arrival, the dads gave me a speakerphone call from their office, wanting to make a special request for their arrival. As they were arriving on a major stat holiday, nothing was open and most people would be busy with their families, so it was unlikely that they would be able to do any shopping of any sort. They wanted to ensure that they would have some of "BC's finest," as they put it, at the lodge for them to enjoy once they arrived. Because I was a regular wine drinker and always had many bottles around, this was not going to be any problem at all so I told them not to worry, that I always had it on hand and would be sure to have some here for their arrival.

It never occurred to me that they meant marijuana. I don't smoke pot; I tried it when I was a kid, but it made me throw up every time, so it quickly lost its charm for me and I never got into it. A doctor once told me that I was probably allergic to it, which caused my adverse reaction, but whatever the reason was it didn't matter—anything that was guaranteed to make me barf was never going to become a part of my life.

An interesting thing with pot is that people who smoke it have this notion that it's a good thing—you know, OK in the eyes of society, mind-opening, thought-provoking, and practically legal. (Most of these stories were written LONG before even the talk of legalization of marijuana in Canada)

They equate it to having a drink and tend to look at you sideways if you give them any grief at all on the subject. In groups where there are a few pot smokers, it's like YOU are the outcast if you don't smoke it. It's hard to describe, but it's like they're completely turned around on the subject; white is now black and black is now white. I have known lots of people who smoke pot and have watched how they change, both short- and long-term. One minute they're lucid, alert, rational, intelligent people, and the next minute they're Spicoli from *Fast Times at Ridgemont High*. (For those unfamiliar, this is an excellent flick from a great decade for movies - the 1980's - about a bunch of high school kids growing up too fast. Spicoli is a bit of a loser surfer who's so wasted that his eyelids are always at half-mast, with mouth hanging partially open. He doesn't understand most things said to him, his laugh is more like a duuuuhhhh – huuuh – huuuuh in really slow motion, and his mind is mostly occupied with fantasies of his own greatness.)

It's like you turn the speed dial from med-high to low when you see what instantly happens to someone who just smoked a joint. They don't realize it; they think they're getting in touch with the universe and are magically developing the insight to solve everything when in the (not red) eyes of the (not smoking pot) observer, they're simply stoned and a bit ridiculous. As the years of pot smoking burn on, slow and stupid "Spicoli" becomes the more common personality of pot-smokers, and over time the other one gets permanently wiped away. I don't care if people want to smoke pot; you can't smoke it in my house, but it's your brain and you can destroy it any way you like. I will likely never change my mind on the subject; the shit rots your brain. That's enough about my thoughts on pot and time to get back to the story.

When my guests arrived, I immediately had an uneasy feeling from them. As I introduced myself, the dad looked at me without a smile; he looked unimpressed and borderline pissed off. I thought, "It's me who should look sour, you overweight, unkempt, sweaty man who hasn't seen a haircut since the 1990's." While he gave me an uninterested introduction to his entourage, the other dad was looking at a collage of pictures that I had of my friends and me on my wall. He turned to me and demanded "How come all of your friends are blonde?" First of all, he was full of crap; not all my friends are blonde, but it happens to be that there are a lot of blondes in that collage, NOT ALL, but majority for sure, so I replied, "Well, I guess I never gave it much thought, but there are a lot of blondes in that frame." Slowly shaking his head, with a nasty tone of sarcasm, he said, "Boy, that must be a room full of stupid."

I'm not kidding, that is verbatim what the pudgy, pasty little asshole's first words to me were when he stepped into my home. I was a bit surprised, but without hesitation I calmly pulled off a great zinger with exactly the same tone. "You're single, aren't you?" was all it took for me take back the power. What made it so perfect was that I could tell by the expression on his face that

I had struck a chord of truth to which he couldn't come up with anything to say, so he just stood there looking dumbfounded. I loved that moment and I will look on it fondly forever. Sadly, thinking back on their stay, the only other fond moment that I recall was watching them leave. But here again, I'm getting ahead of myself, and as the Baroness said, "Dennis would have hated that."

It would seem that I would not be falling in love with either of the adults in this group (a bit of an underestimate!). The three boys seemed like normal teenagers at first, but I was yet to see their true colours. I showed them all to their rooms and they spent a little time unpacking and getting comfortable.

When they emerged from their rooms, the group gathered in the great room. It was evening and I was thinking that I could use a drink, as I felt terribly uncomfortable with the first few moments of the stay and I had a feeling that the awkwardness, along with their attitudes, would not improve.

As I was debating opening a bottle of wine, the father asked me in a loud voice, "So, when are you going to break out BC's finest?" "Great timing! I was just thinking the same thing; I'll be right back with some" I said as I headed up the stairs to my private bar to pick out a bottle that I thought he might enjoy: big, bold, and something that I had a few of in case he could pound back the booze like he looked like he could. I brought it down, showed him the bottle, and asked "What do you think of this one?"

"Yah, sure, I'd have a glass of wine if you're opening it," he shrugged, but then added (and don't forget that this is right in front of his three kids) "What about the weed? I thought you went to get it. You know, BC's finest, isn't that why you went upstairs?"

I stopped dead in my tracks, and I don't think anything could have surprised me more at that moment than the shock of the misunderstanding coupled with the fact that he said it right in front of his kids! Now they were all there, staring at me with great looks of concern on their faces and not saying a word.

This was weird, and it occurred to me how funny my misunderstanding had been, which caused me to burst out laughing hard. I said, "I've always thought that BC's finest was WINE!" and I continued laughing as I started to recover from the shock and open the bottle. As I did so, I realized that nobody else was laughing and they were all still staring at me.

"We thought you were getting us smoke and we don't have any with us," the big daddy informed me, looking very pissed off now.

I thought "So what? That's neither my problem nor my concern." Of course, I had to come up with something a little more tactful than that, so I said, "I'm sorry that I misunderstood you, but I don't smoke pot so I don't buy it and I don't know anything about it. Because of that, coupled with the fact that it's against the law, I wouldn't buy it for anyone else either. When you go out on your tour tomorrow, ask your guide if he has any ideas on getting pot. The guides out here are the eyes and ears of everything, and he'll know who you can call, but I don't even know that because I haven't smoked pot since I was a teenager."

"I can't sleep if I don't have a joint before bed," big daddy blasted me with. He was TOTALLY pissed off at me and, scanning the room; they all were.

Little daddy hopped into the conversation to add, "I thought you understood exactly what we meant—that's what BC's finest means!"

"Not in my world, my friend!" It was the truth and a very honest misunderstanding. "I came to be here after a career in the BC wine industry. Fruit and wine are huge export products for BC and that expression is commonly used in those industries."

At this point, he was going to be nothing but an asshole. "Well, that's not what we wanted and now we've got nothing and I'm not going to get a good sleep, so I'll feel like shit tomorrow." This dude was going to make my life hell until he got a bag of weed.

I couldn't believe that he was guilting me out for not buying street drugs for him. Oh, and the kids were all still standing there listening in complete silence. I felt like I was in the Twilight Zone and wondered how I got there and how in the hell was I going to get out. Perhaps it was my "hostess with the most-ess" desire to make the customers comfortable and happy, or it could have been my need to make this horribly weird situation end, but right at that moment I had a thought that came right out of my mouth, "I'll see if I can help. I'll be back in fifteen minutes," I said as I was pulling on my boots and parka.

At the time, on the awful little rental property next door lived an excellent little Newfie who worked for me part-time doing housekeeping work. I knew she smoked pot and thought she might have an extra joint on hand. As I traveled through the deep snow towards her cabin, I shook my head as I could not believe what I was doing at that moment.

When I got to her cabin and told her the story, she laughed her head off as she rolled a joint for them. As I left, I asked her what she wanted for it, and she said to tell them to leave a good tip for the housekeeper. And so, there I was, with drugs for the guests in my pocket and I would be handing them over in exchange for a bit of money. Great, now I'm a dope dealer, I thought as I wondered how that might look on my otherwise impressive resume.

As I walked back to my home, I thought it best to block it out; this group was on night one of a five-night stay, and it had begun horribly. This might be the only way to get things semi-normal until they could secure themselves with a bag of weed so that they might be able to enjoy themselves on this vacation.

When I walked into the house, they were all still exactly where they had been when I left, and they all gave me a very cold stare.

"OK, here," I said as I proudly offered them the joint, "I got this from a neighbor who just happened to have a little on hand. Enjoy!"

Big Daddy's stare turned to an angry frown as he demanded, "One fucking joint? That's it?"

Now I was starting to get mad, but I held my composure as I responded, "Yes, that's it, that's the best I can do and that's all I'm going to do, so until you make your own drug arrangements, I guess you'll just have to suck it up."

He seemed to back down; he must have been able to tell that I was either on the verge of verbally ripping him a new one or slapping him in front of his kids. "Well, I guess if that's all you're going to do, then we're screwed."

I couldn't let it go, so I gave him a curt and cold reply, "Yah, that's all I'm going to do; drug dealing is not my thing, so you'll have to work it out with someone else." I could not believe this experience was unfolding the way that it was, and I reaffirmed my conviction by refilling my own and the two daddy's glasses of wine. I put on a happy face and attempted to change the subject with "So, you must be excited to go out on your tour tomorrow and see the mountains from on top of them?!"

My question was totally ignored; Big Daddy turned to Little Daddy and said, "Well, let's smoke half of this and then we'll have the other half before bed."

What happened over the next few minutes made everything that had happened up to this point seem very normal...

Big Daddy picked up the joint and pulled out a lighter. He was going to light it right there, sitting at the kitchen island bar.

"Hey," I said, "there's no smoking in the lodge. There are ashtrays on both decks outside."

He shot me a death-stare and declared, "That's total bullshit; we smoke in our house," to which I matter-of-factly replied, "This is not your house, it's mine. It's also a public accommodation and due to allergies as well as health-board regulations, there's no smoking inside." Total Twilight Zone!

And with that, the family put on their coats and boots to go outside to smoke the pot. That's right, the kids too! As they closed the door behind them, I had to physically push my jaw back up so my mouth would not be in the gape position. Oh my god, I thought, this is so bizarre and it's only the first night!

Before I could regain my composure once again, I heard a screaming match breaking out on the front balcony between Big Daddy and one of the kids. Within a few seconds, the youngest son threw the door open, bolted in, slammed the door so hard that the log walls shook as did all of the artwork on them, then ran up the stairs so fast that by the time I was shouting at him to take it easy on the building, with a deafening bang he had slammed his bedroom door too and obviously did not register my message.

The rest of the family was on their way back in through the front door, and Big Daddy must have been made aware of my concern (by the look of appall that was contorting my face), so he offered me an explanation for the tantrum: "Junior's pissed off because we won't share the rest of the joint with the kids."

I was so stunned by this that I couldn't even react, and as it turned out I didn't have time to. The kid came out of his room and started throwing things at his dad from the second floor overlooking the great room while screaming out a string of profanities that would make your ears bleed.

I snapped. Nearing irate, I yelled at him, "Stop that right now! You throw one more thing and I'm throwing your ass out the door!" He stopped and looked at me; it was almost like he had been shaken back into consciousness and he calmly came downstairs, picked up the items, and took them back to his room.

I had taken all I could take. With the other two sons still in the room, I addressed the two dads. "Look, this is ridiculous. I'm sick of the pot-dramas and I'm certainly not going to tolerate tantrums like that again. Perhaps you would be better off staying at a different place, but I'm pretty sure there aren't any around that will let you smoke dope inside or put up with this screaming and fighting and throwing their property around. You can think about it and let me know. I can make other arrangements for you, but if you stay you have to start showing me and my home a little more respect than this. I'm going to my office to take care of a couple of things and to make a couple of phone calls." And with that, I took my glass of wine and went upstairs to my suite to cool off a bit.

I came back downstairs a while later to find the family assembled. The kid who threw the tantrum offered me a sincere apology for his behavior. The dads declared that the family would continue their stay at my lodge, but did not offer any apology of their own.

For the most part, the rest of their stay was surprisingly drama-free.

They got a couple of large bags of dope from somewhere unbeknownst to me, and that seemed to transform them into conflict-free people as long as they all smoked it constantly. It was the strangest thing; without the pot, the whole family was in angry chaos, but as long as they remained stoned, things went relatively smoothly. I felt nothing but pity and contempt for this family; there wasn't much that was "normal" as far as the conventional family unit went. Clearly, those kids were going to have strange lives ahead of them, and I still wonder from time to time how they turned out. I wished they had a mother who could chastise their social offenses and push them toward something more productive than rolling their next joint. "More to be pitied than scorned", my well-used thought, stolen from a sage mother of a friend of mine who uses that phrase very, VERY often.

They continued to nag me about not being able to smoke in the house, and after a couple of days of this I was entirely worn down by them. In the evenings, after all the food had been put away, I would allow them to smoke only cigarettes by the large Jenn Air fan that was built into the island-bar stovetop that sucked the smoke right out of the lodge and to the great outdoors.

Once again, I had sacrificed the "rules" for the sake of the clients and in the spirit of symbiosis. In the end, sometimes you've got to bend a bit, even if it means that you are jeopardizing your own beliefs (not to mention the law!).

When they left, I felt the weight of the world lift from my shoulders. I still can't believe how that first night played out, and many of those images will be forever tattooed into my memory. Strangely, all of the kids gave me a large hug on the way out accompanied by sincere thanks; they seemed to like me, or maybe they just missed their mother, who, by this point I'd surmised, had left them all behind.

A couple of years later, I had another guest who was from the same area as the super dysfunctional family. As he planned his trip, he persuaded me to disclosed Big Daddy's name and business so he could contact him. The new client went to the business to meet Big Daddy. In my next conversation with the new client, I was curious as to what may have been said about me, and so I asked. My guest replied that Big Daddy had said the trip was good, but my new client had gotten the feeling that the dude really didn't like me very much. In my most innocent fashion, I asked him why not, and he told me that it was because I wouldn't let them smoke inside. I laughed my ass off.

· · · · ·

Shit

One dude took a crap in the shower once. Not kidding. After he left, I got into my cleaning routine, looked down, and there in the shower drain was a round poo, blocking the running water. I turned the temperature up high hoping to "melt" it, but eventually had to go find a stick to push it down with. What an asshole! I called him and told him how disgusting he was and to never come back.

·····

The Super Assholes

That's right; the worst of the worst are featured here. If you are reading one of these stories and you say to yourself "Hey, that was me!" then you, my friend, are a Super Asshole and shame, SHAME on you!

·····

How to Hate Women

It was my first full winter at the B&B, as I was still new and very naïve and only had five beds available in only two guest rooms. TR and I had not yet added the additional suite so this was way before the big fire and the giant new lodge. A group of six young men had booked in for several nights, and I had agreed to allow one of them use of the pull-out couch that was in my private living room on the other side of the house when they made their telephone booking and wanted to request separate beds.

To B&B or Not to B&B

They arrived much later than they had promised; my check-in was 4:00-9:00 p.m., and it was around 1:00 a.m. when they arrived drunk at my door after driving across two provinces. My boyfriend and business partner was absent, as usual, so I was on my own to deal with this group of drunken strangers. Oh yes, this was going to be interesting!

One of them immediately plugged an Eminem CD into my stereo and cranked it up. For those of you who are not familiar with the Eminem phenomenon, he's a white rapper who's, angry at everyone—but especially mad at his father and, from what I can tell, all women ("bitches" or "hos" are objectified to the point of terrible abuse in his verbal diarrhea). He uses lyrics like "I shoulda put some anthrax on your Tampax" (sorry—reading that likely made your eyes hurt!) and practically every song is stuffed full of the worst profanities you can think of. If your kid is into Eminem, you might want to take a closer look and consider immediate intervention. (That being said, as the years went by, I came to like a portion of Eminem's music; he's a talented artist when he's not overdoing the shock-value.)

It was the first time I had heard the artist Eminem and I was semi-horrified, but I was new and green to this world, so I blocked it out and tried not to react. If a group of men strutted drunkenly into my home today and plugged an Eminem CD into my stereo, I'd have two words for them before I turned them around and sent them back out the door. Can you even imagine doing that to a woman that you had never met before who was alone in her own home? What the hell was wrong with their heads?

By this time, it was late, so I showed them their rooms and I showed the dude his pull-out up on my side of the lodge. He seemed like the quietest one of the bunch; shy and sheepish, so I thought he liked the idea of being a little bit removed from the rest of the group who seemed to possess a good dose of primate DNA. We'll call him Paul to protect everyone's privacy—though I'm never sure why I have to be so good to them after they were so nasty to me! I said my good-nights and I went into my room, locked the door, and went to sleep.

The next morning when my alarm went off, I put my bathrobe over my pajamas and was making moves to head downstairs to turn on the big coffee urn so it could work its magic while I came back upstairs to get cleaned up and dressed. But as I unlocked my door, turned the handle, and looked up, what do you think I got to see at uncomfortably close range? The idiot who had booked the trip was right outside my bedroom door, facing me with less than eighteen inches separating us, and wearing only his tight red jockey shorts, cowboy boots, and a cowboy hat!

"What the fuck do you think you're doing?!" I angrily whispered at him as Paul was still sawing logs on the pull-out just a few feet away.

He was grinning like he was still drunk from the night before. "I came to check on you to make sure you were OK," was his response.

He was blocking my doorway and now I was confused as well as pissed off. "What are you talking about—why wouldn't I be OK?"

"Because Paul's a convicted rapist." Just like that, matter-of-fact, no big deal.

Now he had my attention, and a deep chill ran through me that felt like ice running through my veins. "You brought a convicted rapist into my home and gave him the bed that's only a few feet outside of my bedroom door?" I angrily demanded.

"Well, it (the rape) happened a long time ago, before I knew him, and he must have changed a lot because he's not like that now so it's probably nothing to worry about."

I was appalled, pissed right off, and shocked by this conversation. I pushed him out of my way on my way to deal with the coffee. "You go put clothes on and you are not to be up here; this is only space for him to sleep, not part of the general space. I am NOT happy about this rapist story you're giving me, but at the moment he's not raping anyone and I have to make breakfast, so we'll have to discuss this later!" I chastised him as I motioned him down to the great room.

The pornographic cowboy followed me down the stairs and into the kitchen, where he lingered in his stupid outfit. I turned on the coffee and told him to go get dressed again, that his attire was unsuitable for being anywhere near frying bacon. Then I went upstairs to wash face, brush teeth, get dressed, and try to calm down my already shot nerves. Paul was still in a deep sleep, so I relaxed a little—after all, he couldn't rape anyone if he was out cold!

They all got up, ate their breakfasts, and headed out for the day. When they returned that evening, they got loser-drunk and became total assholes once again. I didn't feel the need to hang out with them, so after all my clean-up and prep for the next morning was done, I headed to my room for peace and quiet.

Any idea what flannel does to a hot tub?

The next morning when I got up, I discovered that the hot tub was out of service; it had shut itself down with jets and filters clogged with hairy, dark, fuzzy crap. (At a time later, it would be explained to me that the big fat one thought it was necessary to cannonball into my hot tub wearing his flannel pajamas and then stay in there for a while with his pajamas still on.) I would have to call in a repair guy, and who knew how long it would be before the tub would be up and running again and what the price tag for that would look like.

That wasn't the worst of it; they had also left a non-waterproof fabric cooler bag full of ice on my grandmother's antique wooden dining room table whose contents had melted through the fabric. The tabletop was almost completely ruined by water damage and would require extensive repair work. My blood must have gone from the ice-veins to crazy-boil in two seconds flat.

There would be no breakfast. There would be a bill, and there would be an early exodus of this group of assholes, and they would never be back on my property again. By the time they got up, I had their bill ready with several hundred dollars added for damage, and I told them to pack their bags and get out. There were a few protests and a couple of pseudo-apologies, but they reluctantly complied and were soon off my property.

As I stared at the damage and tried to figure out the best plan to try to clean up the mess, it occurred to me that kicking them out wasn't going to be good enough. I went upstairs to my office and sent an email to every accommodation I had on my email list with their names, their actions, and their damage list, and suggested that they be blacklisted from staying anywhere in the area and that there was no way we should be expected to tolerate this kind of behavior from anyone. I hit the "send" button and then went back downstairs to get on with the overwhelming amount of work ahead of me.

A short time later, the phone rang. It was the owner of another B&B up the highway who was calling me to find out if the group of boys on her doorstep had really been kicked out of my place only moments before. Apparently, the assholes were so stupid that they had let it slide out that I had kicked them out and were looking to find a place to stay with her, and she had not yet seen my email. I told her that they had trashed the hot tub and my dining room table and that she would be wise to turn them away. She thanked me for the information, and I could tell she was not going to let them in.

Over the next several days, I received a few return emails from the motels and B&Bs that I had sent the warning to. They expressed great empathy for my situation and thanked me for the valuable information which would put this tribe on their blacklist also, but I wondered if it would truly hold any impact.

I didn't have to wonder for long; a few days after this incident, I received a call from the wife of one of the guys. If truth be told, this guy wasn't bad at all, he was almost likeable and might not have been responsible for any of the damage, but it's one of those situations where guilt by association comes into play. She wanted to straighten this out "woman to woman," as she put it. It quickly became clear to me that she hadn't received the full story; the version she got was more like "The owner didn't like the partying, and thought we were too loud, and there was a small problem with the hot tub." She said that the guys had discovered that they were blacklisted from the area, as they had been unable to book into any other accommodation and were told that they were blacklisted and would never be able to book rooms in the area ever again. This gave me a great feeling of satisfaction and retribution! I told her that this is what happens to people who come to a small community and treat the hosts and their properties with total disrespect.

She suggested that I was overreacting and being unreasonable, and that her husband was a great guy and couldn't have deserved this treatment. I agreed with her that her husband did seem to be fine—but, unfortunately, there were serious problems with others in the group. She didn't believe me and wanted to know what those problems were; clearly, she needed to be tuned in and so I told her the tale, blow by blow. I left nothing out. I wanted to be sure that she understood how it felt to have Eminem, a convicted rapist, and an idiot from a porn-western all in your house in one night when you are there alone and without any back-up. Then I wanted her to appreciate how complicated it is to have major damage repaired in a remote area. I left no details out and shamed her for suggesting that I might be overreacting.

I immediately felt better; this was the best revenge of all! Now all of their wives would know how they behaved when they were unsupervised!

When I was finished talking, she was silent. When she spoke, I could tell the story had slapped her hard in the face. It is my strong suspicion that she had no idea how these men behaved without supervision at all and that she would likely not approve of these behaviors at her home either. The conversation didn't last long after I spilled all of the beans; she got defensive, flustered, and angry to the point that she couldn't even make an argument. After a few verbal shots at me, she hung up. I never heard from or saw any of them again. A great line from Spinal Tap—one of my favorite movies—sums it up. Oh, and you have to say it in a calm and cool British accent:

"We shan't work together again." (A small chuckle from me as I think about the wrath of the wives!)

Incidentally, I only had to kick out two groups from my lodge. That was the first, and the second is coming up in the next story.

. . . . .

Bros & Hos

I don't know how I didn't write this one down immediately after it happened; it's possible that it was so appalling that I couldn't relive it until now, just shy of eleven years later. I don't live there anymore; the place was sold a couple of years ago and I moved far away from all that drama. After I moved away, I began finishing this little writing project and so, as I was going through all the stories, I suddenly remembered the most disgusting of all events in the history of my life as the owner of a B&B. I had successfully blocked it out for so, so long, but in a flash, it was back in my consciousness, as clear as if it had happened yesterday! Without further delay, I will now take you to a far and distant land where nobody from a decent upbringing would ever want to hang out…

The lodge had been rebuilt and TR was, finally, legally out of the picture, and I was exhausted, both mentally and physically. There was the devastation of the total loss fire followed by a two-year rebuild, the semi-dramatic expulsion of TR from my life, and then my exhaustive work and success with all the lawsuits associated with most of the aforementioned. I was freshly off my first winter re-opened, which had been long and filled with many challenges after being out of the game and back into it in a new building with all new equipment.

There was a large project in the small town that would bring many jobs to many people that summer, and would also bring in many transient workers for the entire project time. I took in four of the crew members for the duration of their employment, which promised to be the whole summer. It meant a bit of a sacrifice on nightly jacked-up summer rates in exchange for way less work and guests who would be there for a longer term; it would be a break from the constantly changing roster of people with new faces, names, allergies, dramas, and attitudes. Each of the four got their own room. I was to provide breakfast each morning, fresh towels twice per week, and fresh bed changes weekly. I was looking forward to the "break" and to spending a lot of peaceful afternoons on the golf course while I recuperated from the shit-show that had been my life for the past couple of years.

Two of the crew guys staying with me were fired from the big project within a week of starting. That didn't surprise me at all; these weren't exactly the guys that were going to solve world peace, the common cold, or even a sudoku. I didn't like any of them at all, so to say goodbye to two of the little pricks was enjoyable, except for the fact that revenue was now cut in half. These guys were pond-scum; mannerless and unapologetically crass, insulting, and rude. Burping and farting continuously, language that made my ears feel like they were bleeding; just their presence evoked a sense of disgust in all who had the unfortunate luck of crossing their paths. They were twenty-somethings who were far overpaid for their menial labour, which gave them a spoiled and entitled attitude, and their obvious lack of education made them look and sound stupid. I refer to dudes like that as "repellant" or "chick-off"—yuck, gross!

In the short time it had been since the large project had invaded the small town, I had gotten to know one of the "higher-ups" quite well as we had met on the golf course, had a few cocktails and a few laughs, and became fast friends. He knew all of the idiots who were staying with me and was sympathetic when half of my guests got fired and would be immediately moving out. He said he would do what he could to get me more bookings, as various levels of management were always coming in for a couple of days to check on the progress of the project. Within a few days, he called me to book a suite for a serious VIP and his wife, who would be there for only one night, several days later. It wasn't much, but I was grateful for the booking.

In the meantime, the two dickheads I was stuck with were becoming a huge pain in my ass with their horrible social graces and general clumsiness. They were so rude and disrespectful to me, continually making little insults to my cooking, home, yard, and amenities—which were all fantastic, in case you hadn't already figured that out for yourself.

I had a giant yard; behind the house, patio, garden boxes, and raspberry patch was a cleared stretch of 40m x 150m. It was so big I used to set up a target green and practice pitching shots with my golf clubs back there, up to a seven iron, so you get a general idea of the largeness of space back there.

One day, the shitheads decided to invite a bunch of their worker-buddies over for a game of sort-of-football that was more like passing around a football and making stupid dives to catch it, all while drinking a ton of beer. As said, the yard was, for sure, big enough to accommodate this activity, yet they managed to crash through the raspberries into two of the garden boxes (that were solid log, 2 x 30cm width logs high) and shift them so hard that their plastic liners tore and would cause me enormous effort in containing the dirt within. They didn't apologize or anything; they left me an enormous tip of approximately twenty-four empty beer cans around the yard as a little bonus. I didn't see the cans until the next day, as it was dark when they got hungry and pissed off to town to go find food.

The next day, I picked up all the cans and left them in a pile on the front deck; when they got home from work, I showed them the pile then told them how I had to take a great deal of time to fix the garden boxes and re-tie raspberry bushes that had been knocked down, and clean out the ones that had been broken and killed. I told them this was unacceptable and that if this was how they were going to spend their summer, they should find other accommodations. They thought I was exaggerating and overreacting, though they did apologize, sort of. I was so pissed off I wasn't even interested; besides, the VIP and his wife would be pulling in after dinner, so I wanted to clear my head of these idiots and focus on the other guests who were arriving. I told the idiots that guests were coming and that they had better not disturb them, but they decided they had heard enough from me and took off to town to get fed and drunk at the local bar; the next day was their day off and, by God, they were going to rip it up. I was so infuriated with them that by the time they peeled out of my driveway, I had pretty much decided that I had tolerated enough and that they were going to be evicted the next day. As it turned out, that did happen, but not because of anything you've read about so far...

The VIP and his wife showed up after they had dinner in town. They were so nice, so polite, so gracious, and so happy to have found such a gem of a modern, luxurious, and amenity-filled accommodation in this area that seemed so "rustic" (to put it very politely). We had a glass or two of wine, chatted about this and that, settled on a time for breakfast, bid each other a good-night, and that was that; they went to their suite and I went to mine, clear on the other side of the lodge, far, far away from the guest rooms. I crawled into my cozy bed, inserted the earplugs I had become reliant on for sleeping with noisy guests (and trains!), and fell asleep.

The next morning, I got up and got into the morning routine of preparing the breakfast for the "nice" guests. The shitheads would not have breakfasts on their days off because it was not possible for them to commit to a time that they might be awake, so they would probably sleep off their hangovers as they did on previous days off. If I was lucky, I wouldn't see them until early evening when they were heading out the door for dinner in town.

The VIP and his wife came out of their suite and graciously accepted my offer of fresh coffee as we exchanged good-mornings. I asked them how they slept and was expecting the usual guest reaction of total comfort and blissful sleep, but instead, I got a shocking response that would continue to be added to by other discoveries as the day went on…

"What was going on here last night?" the husband asked me in a quiet but obviously irritated voice.

"What do you mean?"

"The pounding upstairs, the loud music, screaming girls, and the crowd of people up and down the stairs!" he said, followed by, "Didn't you hear it?" in the most incredulous tone ever.

I was so shocked I just froze, staring at him with my jaw dropped; all I could choke out was, "No, I didn't hear a thing; my suite is on the other side of the lodge and I have to sleep with earplugs at night because the trains wake me up." I was trying to get my thoughts together and wrap my head around what I was hearing, so I asked him to tell me everything, detail by detail. As it turned out, the details were not much more than what he'd already given me except to add that this raucous went on for several hours, from somewhere between 1:00 and 4:00 a.m.

It was obvious to me that the VIPs were fully aware that it was their employees who were upstairs by his complete lack of anger. They knew they could not hold me responsible for whatever went down the night before, so I felt more empathy from them than any other emotion. I suspected there were going to be a few behavioral policies added into their employee contracts very quickly! I explained to them that I have my own rules for guests, quiet hours and conduct that they all signed when I wrote up the accommodation contracts with them, so although this was incredibly unfortunate, it was also unexpected. I did, however, assure them that the boys would be "dealt with" for their obvious breach of contract, that they had pretty much worn out their welcome the previous day, and briefly gave them the rundown of how the boys had conducted themselves in my home thus far.

Over breakfast we exchanged a few "crew" stories; it sounded like this sort of disturbance, disrespect, and disorderly conduct was common with stupid young assholes who were out from mommy's wing for the first time. The VIPs had to move along to get to inspecting the work sites and attending management meetings, so they cleaned up and headed out after a leisurely and peaceful morning with me.

After hearing their recount of whatever happened the night before, I made no effort to go on with my cleaning and other household responsibilities in a quiet manner, as I wasn't concerned with disturbing the little pricks as they slept off their bender. I made every effort to do things with loud gusto as I cranked up the tunes to work by. F- them! They had pushed me to a point of pissed-off that they were going to pay for; I was furious.

It seemed strange to me that they weren't waking up; I was making a lot of noise, and for a long, LONG time. I thought maybe they were dead, so I should take a run up to their rooms and find out so that I could at least get their corpses out before they stunk up the joint. I knocked loudly on one of their doors, and even louder on the other ones. No response. I knocked again, this time shouting their names out as doing so. Still no response. Now what?

I turned a handle, opened a door, and was just about knocked over by the stench in the room and realized, immediately, what went down the previous night. I should have taken a picture, but I was so horrified I went into a shocked state of trying to decide what I was going to do about this.

The bedding had been pulled back, revealing the various stains of yellow and brown all over all four beds between two rooms. There were partially drunk beer bottles everywhere, spilled on the beds, carpets, sprayed all over the walls, and a couple that were also used as ashtrays (in my non-smoking house!!). A few of those were also tipped over, adding to the horrible smell. The worst of the worst were the used condoms that were everywhere; and the wrappers all of them torn and leaking lube and whatever bodily fluids were therein contained. There must have been a full dozen condoms that had seen action during the night. It might be a good time to add that I had a very strict "NO GUESTS of GUESTS without the permission of ME" rule written into their contract also! No bodies, alive or dead, anywhere to be seen; the boys had gone out again at some point before I got up to make breakfast, around 4:00 a.m., when the VIPs said the racket had ended.

I immediately went back downstairs and picked up the phone. I called the golf pal who was the "higher-up" project manager on his cell and gave him a brief outline. I must have sounded rather manic because he said, "Don't do anything, I'm on my way." He was there within a few minutes and went upstairs to survey the horror-show that used to be my beautiful guest suites. I could hear the "Holy shit!" escape his breath, and a few minutes later he came downstairs and we decided this was a good time for a large glass of wine.

After administering wine and starting to chill out, it was time to make a plan. "What do you want to do about this?" he asked me, then added, "Anything you want, you have my full support."

I had been forming a solution in my head while we sipped and swapped tales of what a pair of little terds those two were, both at my place and on the job.

"Well, I want them and all their belongings out of my house before 6:00 p.m. today; they are kicked out. The laundry is manageable, though I'm not sure the bedding stains are going to be easily removed, so it could be that there will be new bedding required. Once I get all their disgusting garbage cleaned out, I'm going to be left with walls, floors, and mattresses that will require very deep cleaning. Fortunately, we have a steam-cleaning outfit here that should be able to do all of it. Then, I deserve a medal for not killing them, but I'll take a large cash bonus instead." Depending on the cost of the steam cleaning, the bill for their bad behavior was going to be a few thousand dollars.

With zero hesitation, he said that he would take care of all of it; he was going to haul their asses into the office, rip them wide open, and pull out the cash. To add a little insult to injury, I told him that the one dude's mom had to pay the first week's rent for him, so I had her name, phone number, and VISA number. He smiled and said, "Oh, this is going to be fun!" and then he asked me if I wanted them to be fired; I said that it would be a good threat but that none of this behavior was at the workplace, so I didn't expect it. He was grateful that I was so understanding, as he had told me that it was pretty hard to get as many guys on the project as they needed because so many had already lost their jobs due to their workplace incompetence. When we finished the wine, he went to go gather up the little pricks and haul them in for an ass-chewing, and I called the steam cleaner who was going to be able to come the next day.

I then put on the thickest pair of rubber gloves I owned, my "toilet-cleaning" bracelet (private joke!), and a face mask, and began picking up and stripping down the rooms. I gathered up all the condoms and put them in pockets and corners of their duffle bags, as with the cigarette butts that were soaked in beer and other fluids in glasses. All of their clothes that were laying around were used to clean and soak up spills on the bedside tables, windowsills, walls, and flooring, then tossed into the duffle bags, which were tossed onto the front deck with the empty beer bottles in the empty cases on top of them. All of their toiletries and personal items from the bathrooms were put into a plastic bag and tossed onto the deck too. All of their belongings were sitting out there, ready for them when they got back.

Their arrival home, and their almost immediate and final departure, was uneventful. I was sitting on the deck with a glass of wine and my hand held out as they approached, "Your keys, please," was all I said. They handed the keys over, began a lame form of apology, and I just gave them the hand, told them I didn't want to hear it, did not care, and that the only thing I wanted from them was their absence in my life. They had a quick look around for any items that may not have been gathered up for them, and then they left. The End? Not quite, LOL.

My friend, their boss, came over for a drink or two the next day. As it turned out, he was a better friend than I thought, because he decided to really punish these jerks. Earlier that morning, he hauled their asses into his office and scolded them, loudly and harshly, like a parent would after discovering their child had beat up another kid in the playground. He topped it off by telling them that if they wanted to keep their jobs, they would agree to have a large amount of money deducted from their pay to cover cleaning and distress they had caused me. To pour more salt into their wounds, he told them that they would be on probation for three months each, and one single action they took that damaged the reputation of the company would result in not only their termination from employment, but also that he would personally call their mothers to tell them what kind of "men" they were turning out to be! I still laugh about that whenever I think about it!

. . . . .

Chapter 8 - Outside Forces

As a lodge owner, you may start out having zero clue as to how many things affect your business that you would think have nothing to do with your business at all. This set of stories will give you a pretty good idea of how what other people do has a direct impact on your show, which you may have (stupidly) thought would be entirely under your control alone. Ha!

. . . . .

The Neighbors

It has to be pointed out that when you operate a B&B, your neighbors can play an important role in your guest experience. Disruptions and disturbances from the surrounding properties can affect your ratings and reviews, and this ultimately can sway your success one way or another.

Sue Marko

One of the properties that shared a property line with me was owned by a couple of local upper-middle-aged sisters. The property had several small dwellings on it that the sisters rented out, mostly to young folks but practically always (with only two exceptions that I can remember) to "problem" people. In reflection, it reminds me of that series *Trailer Park Boys*, but with much less organization and motivation. It got to the point that I wouldn't even bother attempting to meet and form a decent neighborly relationship with newcomers to that property because it almost never failed to be a huge waste of my time.

When I first moved in, I should have been a little more receptive to the gigantic red flag that was waving right in my face. At that time, and for many years, two of the dwellings were occupied by a family: a husband and wife with three little kids (all in a one-bedroom unit!) and the husband's brother with a roommate or two in the other. The adults were all pleasant, kind people who would, no doubt, try to help out in a time of need, but they held one stand-out characteristic from the get-gobthat became unbearable by the end of their occupancy—they were slobs. (The children were a nightmare, but because they were little kids, they were likely a product of their environment and so will remain untouched here.)

I had to drive past their dwellings through the access to my property, and it never failed to shock me that the state of their yard got worse and worse and WORSE as time passed. It looked like they were having a yard sale every single day; the yard was always littered with kid's toys, garbage, and general clutter. This was accentuated by the fact that they, like almost every one of their successive renters, didn't bother with even the most rudimentary yard work. Not that they could have cut the grass; there was too much crap laying all over the place for that. It was embarrassing, especially because my guests, too, had to pass that "disaster" and routinely commented on the fact that it was too bad my beautiful place was situated beside such a slum. Their crap was even up in the air; they insisted on using a clothesline to exhibit their laundry, including their well-used underwear.

There was always talk (hope!) of them moving, as they were building a home down the highway, but it was years before they would make good on their talk. Finally, the whole family moved out and took all of their toys, junk, and laundry with them. There was a brief spell of serenity on that unoccupied property, but it didn't last.

·····

Police Intervention

Unfortunately, the local RCMP became quite familiar with my property. It was never because of anything that I did, precipitated, or could even have prevented; nevertheless, they were out there many times over the years. Interestingly, with the exception of the time that they had to come to my property to verify that the extensive damage to the front of my truck was caused by a suicidal deer, the authorities were frequent attendees due to routine incidents at that "trailer park" property next to me.

There was a grow-op busted there, parties broken up regularly, and at least one break-in that I remember; their property was never recovered, and it's a real shame because a family heirloom was included in the items that were stolen. By the way, the couple who were the victims of the break-in were the ONLY people that lived on that property in over fourteen years that I considered my friends. There was one French-Canadian dude who helped me with renovations whose company was well enjoyed but he was there for such a short period of time that we didn't become friendly enough to stay in touch. All others are now, much to my content, absent from my life.

In my youth, I was on the wrong side of the law a few times, but since growing out of that rebellious (and stupid) phase I have learned that the police/RCMP are around for good reason and that you never know when you are going to need their help, so it's a smart move to be on their good side at all times. This is particularly true in a small town where everyone knows everyone. This is also particularly true when you are a single female living several kilometers away from the town on a large, secluded property by yourself.

One incident was particularly frightening for me...

A gal a little bit younger than myself moved into the property who, at first, was a welcome addition to that place. She was from an underprivileged background and had led a very hard life but still managed to always be cheerful and optimistic for the future. She always worked hard, taking difficult and low-paying jobs of housekeeping long hours to cover her bills. I hired her to work for me in my busy periods, as she was a terrific housekeeper and enjoyable to spend time with. We'd chat every day and we would often get together to play card or dice games and tip back a few beers in the evenings. She would tell me stories of her previous gypsy lifestyle in Eastern and Central Canada, and it always amazed me further that she was such a happy person; her experiences of abuse and hardship were beyond anything that I could imagine, and would not be easy for her to recover from. She was immaculate (although she pronounced it "immaculant") in her work, home, and yard. She had a very big heart and she was great company during the lonely off-seasons; I would go so far as to say that she became acceptable as a neighbor—but one that would be in my life for only a brief time. Her downfall? She had giant and potentially deadly baggage.

Her baggage came in the form of a big, biker, bully, bastard boyfriend who was also a recovering crack addict and alcoholic. I am not kidding or exaggerating one bit. He was only there for a day or two each week, as he was a long-haul truck driver. He scared the crap out of me, and it's important to note that there are not a lot of things that scare the crap out of me but he sure did, especially once he started hitting the booze. He was unpredictable and violent; I could always tell when he had been drinking because I could hear him shouting at her from inside my extremely well-insulated house, and it would often be coupled with loud bangs and crashes when he would start throwing things around and breaking stuff on that property next door. I would always see her within a day or two, and she would say things like "Oh yah, he got into the booze and the asshole came out. He broke the screen door right off when he slammed it, but then he passed out and started apologizing the second he woke up and swore that was the last time he would drink." This pattern of drug and alcohol fueled rage followed by next day, semi-sober apologies happened every other time he came home, if not every time.

On one very hot day in July, he started hitting the booze mid-morning. His daughter was visiting for a short holiday and the reunion was stressful and not going well for them. The daughter had every addiction and personality disorder that her father did, and she was, without any doubt, one of the scariest, sketchiest, dirtiest, sleaziest young women I've ever met. I could see that the "family" time was going to get dysfunctional, to say the least. I popped over to their place around 10:00 a.m. to bring an item back to my gal-pal that I had borrowed. Father and daughter had already had an argument revolving around the local boy the daughter brought home to have sex with the night before, and now both were into the alcohol out of frustration. My gal-pal was upset because of that argument but also because she'd had an argument about wanting the daughter there at all; she didn't, at all, and that didn't go over well with dad. So, they were all mad at each other and two of them were on their way to wasted.

They were having a barbeque later that day and had previously invited me to join them. My friend was busying herself making preparations for the dinner to avoid the other two until everyone had cooled off and they were ready to enjoy the beautiful day. I quietly suggested to her that this might not be a good day for me to come over and that she should get out of there too, as things might escalate rather than cool off. She insisted that the dinner go on and that I come, so I reluctantly agreed to come back for the barbeque after I had done all my various things. I didn't want to have anything to do with them that day; nobody wants to be around angry, aggressive, and abusive drunks, but I felt so sorry for my friend's desperate plea for my company that I couldn't refuse her.

I arrived in the early evening heat with a beer in hand. It was worse than I thought. "Drunk" doesn't describe it; dad and daughter were "loser-drunk." You know, babbling, stumbling, eyes going in different directions, loud and indecipherable words and phrases belting out, and without any control over any of their actions. Likely, there would be no recollection of any of it either. The father-daughter fight was in full swing again, but now my friend had consumed many drinks also and was contributing provoking little sentiments like "whore," "slut," "crackhead," and so on. It didn't take me long to figure out that I was leaving, going into my house, and locking the doors; this was something I wanted NOTHING to do with. And so, after dispute from my pal, I was able to pull myself out of there and to the sanctuary of my own property.

Over the next several hours, I could hear the yelling and crashing that had become so routine from that property. It was making me sick and I thought I should call the RCMP to have them throw the bunch of them in the tank for the night to make myself feel easier, but as this was going through my mind the noise seemed to be quieting down. Within half an hour or so, things had pretty much settled down, so in the relief of the newfound peace I felt very tired; I began turning out lights and making all preparations to go to sleep and then went up to my room to get into bed.

As I got upstairs, I could hear someone running up the steps of my front porch, immediately followed by frantic banging on the front door. I knew without even one doubt that it was my friend and that she was in big trouble. I raced down to the main floor to let her in and I could hear her crying and shouting for me to open the door while she continued pounding on it. I grabbed the cordless phone on the way.

I unbolted the lock and ripped the door open to see my friend standing there screaming and bleeding from various locations that I couldn't identify right away. I pulled her in, slammed the door and called 911 for my friend as she was in a hysterical state and couldn't speak; her breathing was so erratic that I thought she might be having a heart attack. The operator was sending officers in cruisers to put an end to this night of domestic abuse. While she stayed on the phone with me, she told me to stay in the house and keep the door locked; the police officers would come to my house after they had the situation at the other house under control. The blood was coming from her face and arms, but looked like they were all minor cuts so I assured the operator that I could patch them up while waiting for the RCMPs to come.

What followed next door (as was later recounted to us by the officers) was right out of Hollywood. The officers arrived only to find the dad and daughter attempting an escape in the detached cab of the semi-truck that he drove; like operating a motor vehicle was a good idea in that condition! So, the police chased them for a short way and then he pulled over and both he and his daughter jumped out and started running. The officers were able to catch them, but they put up an enormous fight before they were handcuffed and put in separate police cruisers. Apparently, the daughter was so cranked up on whatever she had been pumping into herself all day that she went nuts inside the police cruiser and kicked out several windows. When the officers showed up at my door, all three were covered with dirt from the fight on the ground, and they had various rips in their uniforms and cuts on their limbs and faces. They were shaken up pretty good, so I imagine it was even scarier than what they described.

By that time, my friend had calmed down and was able to make her statement to them. Around 1 a.m., the officers left us. They were putting the dynamic duo in the drunk tank for the night while they sorted out what all to charge them with. They told her to stay at my place, but because the fight had caused so much damage she wanted to go home and start cleaning up the mess and making a list of what was destroyed so that she could have that list included in the police report.

Eventually they all left me, alone in my beautiful B&B with my head spinning from the day's events and wondering how it would have been if I had guests there. How would that night fit into a perfect vacation plan for unsuspecting and perfectly innocent travelers? Then my thoughts wandered to how it was going to go when he got out; I was the one who called the cops, so was he going to blame me? This last thought stayed with me for months, maybe years.

The father and daughter were both charged with all sorts of crap and were ordered to leave the area with restraining orders against them for both my friend and me, which included the properties that we lived on. I haven't seen either the father or the daughter since. Shortly after this incident, my friend packed up and moved away to start yet another chapter. She wasn't sure where she was going, but she knew that she would never feel safe until she was not on that property, and I knew exactly how she felt.

· · · · ·

The Property Line

My property was beautiful, I mean REALLY beautiful. It was beautiful because I spent so much time making it that way—these things don't just happen; they take work and continual upkeep. I was always doing yard work, as I liked doing it and I believed it to be necessary in adding another element of enjoyment to my guests' visits. In the summer, the acres of lawn were perfectly manicured, flowers were in large planters all over the decks and yard that were watered and dead-headed every day, branches on trees that hung too low were neatly removed, the rockwork was maintained to be free from any debris, the herb and vegetable gardens were weeded continually and planted in perfectly straight rows, and fertilizers were generously used everywhere to promote lush and healthy-looking plant life. In the winter, the snowplowing was exact and the entire yard was left as a pristine white artist's canvas where the only brushstrokes allowed were added by the occasional footprint from a forest creature. I can't even count the comments that I received from visitors who gushed on about what an oasis my property was (especially when compared to the neighbors').

In addition to an ongoing string of tenants who didn't lift a finger to improve the esthetics of the green space, the rental property owned by the local sisters had a continual tradition of property line abusers. I don't know why, but for some reason the occupants seemed to believe in communal access rights or something stupid or pot-induced like that. I suspect that the fact that my property was maintained to park-like standards created a temptation for them to experience its serene beauty for themselves.

One family moved into the A-Frames who thought they, too, would start a B&B, but they lasted less than six months as they clearly had no idea what effort was needed to be made to satisfy not only guests but the Health Board.

They were there less than a month when I had to write them a letter carefully outlining that they were not allowed to snowmobile on my property. The letter followed an event which involved them building an actual snowmobile jump on my property while I was out running errands in town. I pulled into my driveway and my jaw must have hit the steering wheel when I saw what they were doing without my permission ON MY PROPERTY. I got out of my car and asked them what they were doing, and to my surprise they said that this was the best place to build it because there was so much room. Stupid or what? Once they figured out that this was not going to be allowed, they became belligerent with me and defiantly stated that "Where we come from neighbors are a little more neighborly, everybody shares!" Really? I'm supposed to share all I've bitten, clawed, and scraped to own with a tribe of backwoods hillbilly renters? And can you believe the nerve of these rubes? Seriously? Building a jump on my property, adjacent to my driveway, in direct view of my picture window so that they could do something so stupid and dangerous while destroying the perfect snowscape that was MY property. "Where do these people come from?", I wondered.

Pretty much par for the course; no respect for the nice lady next door who actually owns the property that she lives on.

The summer after those people moved out, they were replaced with a family that had "noise" drama. Everything about them was noisy; they had a kid that seemed to be able to communicate only through screams (I got to be able to tell the happy screams from the angry screams), they had a nasty little Chihuahua or similar breed that yapped incessantly, and even their vehicles were of the unmaintained breed, so they sounded a little more like farm equipment than cars when entering and leaving the property.

Their noisiness irritated me, but not so much as their non-acknowledgement of the "boundaries" that existed not only for humans but also for the humans' dog. I saw the kids riding their bikes on my driveway a couple of times, but that's no big deal; no harm and no foul. BUT that nasty little dog of theirs was free to wander, to poop and to dig and to generally drive the next-door neighbor nuts with its very presence. Every time I saw it on my property, I would clap at it and chase it back to its own yard and its owners would immediately send it inside where it would have to suffer a "time-out."

One perfect day right at the end of June, I was having a glass of wine on the front porch with a good friend of mine. We were watching the latest barrage of robins gather worms and other delectables for the young in their nests, which were scattered around my property. It was a banner year for robins; I had at least five nests which contained at least twenty babies. I respected their space and insisted that all visitors of my property do the same and make use of binoculars or camera zooms if close-up viewings were desired.

Out of nowhere the shitty little dog comes ripping across the front of my yard past the deck where we were sitting, in an unexpectedly violent attempt to capture a robin that was in process of extracting a worm from the lawn. Without any hesitation, I was on my feet and sprinting toward the dog while yelling to alert the bird so it could escape to safety. The robin blasted off, and the shitty little dog was left there, yapping and snarling at the robin in flight.

I was irate and was going to pick up the shitty little dog and relocate it back into its own yard, but the thing turned on me and started snapping and lunging at me. This made me even madder and I charged at it, but it was not backing down. I thought, "OK, bite me. Then I'll have a case against you to take to animal control." I turned and stomped all the way to their house, right to the front steps of their porch with the shitty little dog yapping and snapping at me the whole way there.

The mother appeared and I demanded, "Is this your shitty little dog?" She answered, "Yes." "Well, your shitty little dog was just in my yard trying to kill birds! You either keep this thing inside your house or you keep it tied up in your yard at all times from now on. Do you understand?!" "It's okay!" she emphatically stated (there may have been language/translation issues going on here). "NO, it's NOT okay—if it were okay, I wouldn't be standing here yelling at you! You put that thing on a leash right now and you keep it on a leash from now on, or there are going to be real problems for you. Do you understand?!" (Oh yeah! I was mad enough to make threats). "Yes, yes, it's okay," she said again. I had said (yelled) what I needed to say, and without any further interaction, I stomped back to my property to rejoin my friend. I didn't see the shitty little dog for a day or two after that.

On Canada Day, I was out in the yard doing the usual tasks of primping, preening, and watering the flowers. On this day, I included watering the three little spruce trees that my dad and I had planted the previous summer. We had planted those three trees dissecting the line of sight between my front porch and the porch of the shitty little cabin where the shitty little dog lived, in hopes that one day the trees would block the presence of other occupants in this part of the world. The three little trees were on my property, within ten feet or so of the property line. The back porch of the shitty little cabin that the shitty little dog and its family lived in was within ten feet of the property line going the other way.

To my horror, there lay a perfect little dog poop right beside one of my little spruces. My blood was on instant-boil, and without any hesitation I was on a mission. I knew what had to be done; words hadn't worked on this tribe, so it was now the time for action. In a calm and fluid motion, I put down my watering can and strode toward the shop to grab my weapon, and then headed back to the crime scene. I carefully slid the shovel underneath the shitty little dog's poop and picked it up in one piece, without disrupting its form or integrity. I then tiptoed the gift over to the family's back doorstep and carefully laid it right where someone's foot would land if exiting the building without looking down.

I laughed my ass off about that little bit of payback, and it still gives me a giggle when I think back on it today. Interesting to note that after this happened, the shitty little dog was never seen on my property again. When I would be over on that side of my yard tending to the flowers, trees, or grass, I would often see it tied up on a leash in front of their house. It would see me and always start yapping angrily, like it felt like I was to blame for its newfound incarceration; this always brought me a great deal of satisfaction and amusement.

. . . . .

Various Irritations from the Other Side

For most of my years at the B&B, the other side of my property had no neighbor issues because it had no occupants. It was a property of forest separating my property from the train tracks. A couple of years before I sold my property, that property on the other side was purchased by a woman who was not local. In the late fall, she started cutting all those trees down. I didn't get it—WHY would a person do this? I thought she must be nuts, so, as I did with the rental property on the other side, I tried to ignore her and her activities and stick to myself and my own beautiful property.

Unfortunately, it was difficult to ignore this woman and her tree-cutting, as it became more apparent how much I was being affected by her actions. All those thick trees had provided great insulation from both the sound and vibration of the trains. The more trees she cleared, the louder the trains became; but worse, I could FEEL them in my house now. Not so much on the main floor but very noticeable on the second floor; every time a train went by, the upstairs would shake a little. On average, there were forty trains each day, so from that point on, every time I felt a train go by, I disliked that woman a little more.

Shortly after she practically clear-cut her property, she pulled into my property in her pick-up. It was the first time I had a look at her as she introduced herself to me. I immediately labeled her as a bit of a hippy-type. She looked like she was in pretty good shape for her fifty or so years, and was dressed in "young girl" clothes that were clean enough, yet she seemed unkempt; disheveled hair, wrinkly clothing, and she was in a state of confusion and spininess that I would discover was her normal state of being. Because of my ongoing experiences of bad neighbors, I was cool with her and did not make any effort to encourage a friendship; I listened to her blather on about how she wanted to create an "artists' retreat" where art enthusiasts could come and camp and paint or whatever. This didn't appeal to me at all, as it sounded like a commune for pot-smoking, dirty hippies who held "kumbaya" sing-alongs until the wee hours of the morning while waiting for the tail of a comet to hop on—and how lucky for me to live next door. Yuck.

I was wondering when she was going to leave me to my privacy again when she got around to doing what she had come to do: ASK ME A FAVOR. Great! This is exactly how I would LOVE to start off another crappy relationship with someone who, in all likelihood, was another crappy neighbor. "I'm going on the bus to meet my mother and we're going on a train and to the island and (blah, blah, blah, blah, blah...) and I was wondering if I could leave my truck on your property for the ten days I'll be gone, because it would be much safer here than on my property where there is nothing or nobody there." I thought, "No kidding there's nothing there!" with not a tree left in sight thanks to your genocidal project. "Well, I've got customers here in two weeks, and I need all of my parking spaces as they are bringing two large trailers and at least two large trucks, so as long as you have it out of here in ten days, then I don't mind if you leave it here." She replied, "Oh, no, I promise I'll be back in ten days and it will be gone before your guests arrive."

Three weeks later, after the group of guests had come and gone, I was still looking at her F-ing truck in my guest parking spaces but with close to three feet of snow on it by then. It was a few days later that the truck magically disappeared while I was in town running errands. A small box with what I thought was homemade toffee or fudge laid on my front door mat, with no note of apology for the imposition or anything to express her acknowledgement of her breaching our agreement, nothing except the box with the unidentified brown blobs in it. In the back of my mind,

I remembered the flash of the dirty hippies, but this time I imagined them making hash brownies. I walked into the kitchen and dropped the box of unidentified brown blobs into the garbage and wrote off yet another neighbor.

With the break of spring, construction commenced on that property; someone told me that she was building a small cabin and I couldn't care less. That is, until the construction noise became ridiculously intrusive with the cutting of the metal roof at 6:00 a.m. while my paying guests (paying for serenity and privacy) were trying to sleep. I was pissed off, so I did what anyone would do; I called my buddy the municipal building inspector, who also happened to be the local representative for the Regional District in which I lived. I told him about the construction noise and how disturbing it was. At first, he was confused and he asked me what kind of construction this was, so I told him. He then became agitated and said that there was no building permit issued for that property! Busted! He pretty much hung up on me as he was in such a twist to get out there and see what was going on WITHOUT A PERMIT. I saw his truck driving into the road within five minutes, which was pretty good speed considering that our properties were six km from his office. Later that day, he called me to tell me that indeed, the construction was not only unpermitted but what they had done so far was not meeting any building code, so he'd slapped a stop-order on it. Construction immediately ceased and would not be resumed until that kooky hippy sold the property nearly five years later. That was my very last interaction with her, and I've got to say,

I felt good to be done with her and it brings a smile to my face every time I think about her getting shut down then moving out.

A year or so later, I heard that she and her boyfriend had broken up and "The War of the Roses" ensued over there, resulting in him driving a piece of heavy equipment right over their expensive and perfect deck in an effort to undo his contribution to the project. After that, I don't think she even spent time next door; I thankfully saw no evidence of her presence ever again.

One day, out of the blue, that property was then purchased by a great couple from Alberta who planned to transform it into their vacation oasis. I liked them and liked hanging out with them, but my property sold shortly after they took possession and before I had a chance to become friends with them. They were the only good property-line sharers I ever had there, and for the very shortest and very last time.

· · · · ·

The Jerk Who Owned the Property Behind Mine

There was a small hobby farm on the property behind mine; we did not share a road or a property line, thank God, because of all the neighbors over all of the years, I liked the dude who owned that property THE VERY LEAST. My encounters with this guy over all that time were unpleasant at best, and were often nothing short of completely infuriating.

When I bought the property, the little farm was owned by an elderly woman who was one of the founders of the community and was an integral part of the beginnings of the tourism industry in that area. I barely got to know her at all, as it wasn't long after TR and I took over the property that she moved on. She had been the perfect neighbor, occasionally seen and never heard; in other words, she didn't do anything to piss me off.

The property was sold to a man and his wife who had lived in the community for years. They made a lot of noise; their theme was "burnin' gas and kickin' ass." Everything they owned was an environmental and audial assault, and they disturbed my guests and me often. Over the years, I endured their awful tractors, snowmobiles, ATVs, and his "work" vehicle (loudest possible vehicle ever invented!) which drove to and from town every day VERY early in the morning and then again to and from town later in the afternoon Monday to Friday. To top off all of this, they insisted on having roosters! Right? I know what you're thinking: "Maybe they were hard of hearing?" If they weren't before all this crap, they must have become that way by now! Have you ever had a rooster next door? Let me tell you that it's possibly the worst possible thing one could hope for, especially in the late spring when it's getting hot outside, all the windows are open, and the sun is starting to come up around 5:00 a.m. I can't even tell you how many times I wanted to go over there and strangle the F-ing rooster and then strangle them.

And so, my dislike for these neighbors was imminent. I supposed that they weren't doing these noisy things specifically to piss me off; more likely they were ignorant to anyone else's experiences of their actions and choices. But then there came a point when the fellow took a jab at me that could be interpreted in no other way than that he, like many others, resented my successes and was likely more than happy to cause me difficulty and expense.

. . . . .

"Sometimes it's Hard to be a Woman" (Tammy Wynette)

The hobby farmer and his wife had been living there for a couple of years and we were still at a point where we were cordial to each other; we would waive or smile, say hi and exchange a few pleasantries when our paths crossed. My business was doing OK and my property was a big focus for me, as I had finished building the lodge, all the decorating was done, and at this time I did my best to make improvements to the yard, garden, and the outlying property features. This included mowing most of the four acres that I owned using the lawn tractor that I owned.

One day the mower died. I called "the mower guy" who was a fantastic local cowboy with a great sense of humour, was the best small engine repair dude on the planet (as far as I was concerned), and dealt with his clients more like they were friends than someone he could get money out of, which unfortunately was common treatment by most people you would pay for a service in that community. He came over, had a quick look, and told me that it didn't look like anything simple and that I should make other arrangements for cutting my grass. He loaded up my little tractor and I didn't see it again for a few weeks.

I called up the hobby-farmer neighbor to see if I could borrow his, as this seemed like the most sensible solution and it was right across the little road at the back, so it was very convenient.

"Oh geez, I don't think so" was his response, to which I asked "Why not?" He said, "Well, I don't think you know how to operate a lawn tractor." "Of course I do; I own one and have owned one for years!" I replied, in total surprise. "Well anyways, you probably don't know how mine works." It's just a lawn tractor, it ain't rocket science, you stupid hillbilly—was what I wanted to say—but I could tell by the tone in his voice that he was not about to believe that a GIRL could operate one of his machines. That was that, he was not going to loan his precious machine to me. I called around and found my only option was to hire someone to do it.

The first guy I hired quoted me $350 at first. WTF!? I told him that was ridiculous and that it only took me two hours to cut the whole thing, so his rate of $175/hr was never going to be met by me. I called a couple of others; one was out of town and the other's machine was broken. I found one more guy who would do it with a push mower, but I would supply the push mower, all the gas, and pay him $15/hr cash. I couldn't imagine how long that would take; it seemed like it would be comparable to the outrageous rate the initial prick quoted me. This was shockingly unreasonable and I felt like I was being hosed because 1) I'm a girl; and 2) I was a girl with a big, fancy looking place in a desperate spot.

I was manifesting a serious tantrum when $350-guy roars into my driveway with his tractor on a trailer in tow. I pretended not to notice and made myself busy with my tomato plants, appearing to not even be thinking about the damn grass and how the hell I was going to get it cut. He got out of his truck and walked over behind the house where he saw me.

"Well, I thought I would come over and have a better look at the size of the job," he declared, like he had a divine right to be there and that I should consider myself blessed for him to choose to do so.

"I told you I'm not paying $350. I'd crawl around on my hands and knees and chew it down myself before that happened," I very sarcastically snapped at him. To his credit, he laughed at that. I wasn't laughing, though; I was in a bad mood by this point and I'm sure he could tell.

"Yah, it's really not as big as I thought." After he twisted his grubby neck around each way to scan the yard, he said, "I'll do it for $175."

I stared at him with my best poker face and said, "I'm not paying you $175 either; I'll give you $125." Now he was staring at me, and I just kept staring right back. We settled on $140, and he was off my property in less than two hours and my lawn was done.

I know, that's still way too much money, but my hands were tied, and at that moment I felt like it was the only option I had.

The following week, I borrowed a push mower and called up the guy who charged $15/hr. I didn't realize he was a big pot smoker; pot makes people move slower than normal, so it took him two full afternoons and cost me as much as the other guy, plus I had the added joy of listening to a lawn mower for nine hours. The following week, the small-engine-repair cowboy brought back my mower, and I'm pretty sure it was one of the happier moments in the fourteen years of dealing with the grass that I had. I never again asked for anything from the hobby farmer, as I believed it would have given him too much joy to say no to me again.

· · · · ·

The Farmer's Dog

The hobby farmer always had a dog or two, but they were never a problem for me until one beautiful and warm spring day. I adore dogs; I had the best dog in the world, a Golden Retriever, who was smart, sassy, and a constant source of entertainment, so it's not like I'm a "hater" or anything like that—I like dogs. OK, now that we've got that cleared up…

I had seeded my garden boxes the day before; I had four huge log raised-garden beds that were imbedded in my pristine rock landscape that surrounded the house inside of where the lawn began. The rocks went out up to thirty feet from the house foundation, were underlaid by landscape material that kept the weeds out, and the four boxes were perfectly built towards the rear perimeter, which was clearly and professionally outlined by deeply inlaid landscape border. It was the perfect garden to enjoy from the perfect rear deck or the slate patio in the ground between the deck and the boxes. I sweat blood to make this an oasis for my guests; it was immaculate at all times, and I will always fondly remember many of my summer guests lounging out there with a glass of wine, relaxing music, and not a care in the world. You can imagine that I would be very irritated by any little weed that dared to spring up or anything that deterred from the perfection I had achieved in my backyard.

That morning, I went out into the yard to water my newly seeded, perfect little rows in my perfect garden boxes. A few minutes into the process, movement caught my eye, and loping toward me was a big, beautiful, red-blonde dog not terribly unlike my gorgeous dog (who had passed on years before), so I was immediately made to like this fabulous pooch. I could tell he was on a mission of friendship, so I put down the hose to greet him and he ran right up to me for greetings and a long introduction of licks and pets.

After our friendly session, I said, "OK, that's it, time to go home," and pointed back toward where he came from, which was the direction of the hobby farmer's place. The dog wasn't going anywhere but I had to, so I wanted to make sure he got back to wherever he came from before the sun cooked his pretty little ass. Nope, he wasn't interested, but I was insistent and walked him out to the middle of the yard, urging him to "Go home!" while pointing to where he came from.

He ran back over to my house and laid down in the rocks in the shade, and I thought "OK, do what you like," finishing my watering before I had to leave to run to town to do errands.

When I finished watering, he still wouldn't leave. After a few more attempts, I called the neighbor to see if it was his dog, but there was no answer, so I left a message saying that if it was his dog, he should call it back home. I had no choice; I had to leave the dog there and go do my errands, so I put out a bowl of water for him and headed out.

When I returned, I came back to one horrifying disaster. That damn dog had crawled up into each one of my perfectly organized and seeded garden boxes and dug up every one of them. Dirt was sprayed everywhere and there were craters in every spot that he had frantically pawed at until he moved on to the next one! OH MY GOD, I WAS FURIOUS! I mean, I went from normal to FUCKING IRATE in half a second! And the dog, covered in mud from my wet garden, was lying in the middle of one of the boxes.

Without even thinking about it, I grabbed the phone and redialed the hobby farmer. Again, no answer, so I left a message, a little angry in tone (maybe a lot!) asking again if this dog was his and letting him know that he better come and get it! Then I hung up, skipping any mannerly goodbye.

Not more than ten seconds later, he called back to inform me that yes, it was his dog, and if I didn't want him there, then I should send him home. Really? What a great idea, duh! I told him that I had tried that about twenty times, to which he replied, "Then you should hit him with a stick or something." I was shocked by this and told him that in the world I live in, people do not hit dogs with sticks and that he better call his dog home and keep him there. Then, the hobby farmer said possibly the most stupid thing I've ever heard: "Maybe you should build a fence—it's not my problem if my dog is in your yard."

I surprised myself with my calmness in this moment. I took a deep breath and said, "Listen, here's what's going to happen: You are going to figure out how to keep your dog in your yard as of this moment, right now. If your dog is not off my property in the next few minutes, I'm sure he will have no problem following me into my garage, where I will get him to jump into my truck. Then do you know what I'm going to do?"

Total silence on his end; I'm sure he thought I would say something like "Drive him out into the bushes and shoot him," because that's how people like him deal with problems, but not people like me.

"I'm going to take him directly to the pound, where it's going to cost you $107 to have him bailed out. Then tomorrow, when he comes back, we're going to go through the same exercise, and it's going to cost you another $107 to bail him out. Then we're going to go through that same thing every damn day UNTIL YOU

LEARN HOW TO KEEP YOUR OWN DAMN DOG IN YOUR OWN DAMN YARD!" Yup, I was yelling by the end of it, and then I hung up the phone again, not waiting for any more crap to fall out of his mouth.

Within ten seconds, I heard the whistles and hollers and the dog took off, back home, and I never saw him on my property again. It took me the better part of two days to get my yard back into a state that was suitable for guests, as I had to reseed the entire garden and never once received an apology for the destruction and mess the farmer was ultimately responsible for. I doubt they ever understood what a disaster that was for me and how that careless attitude and behavior could negatively impact my business, but it wasn't nearly as shitty (carefully chosen word) as what was to come.

. . . . .

The Rodeo

Close to a year before I sold the lodge, I got up one morning to pack a bag and go visit my parents for my mom's birthday. I was in the kitchen organizing a cup of coffee, when through my large front window, I was distracted by a very large, dark figure in my front yard. At first glance, I thought it was a moose or a full-grown bear (not a rare sighting at all), but after refocusing my blurry, sleepy eyes, I realized it was a cow!

Confused and irritated, I went over to the front door and opened it. When I looked out, to my horror I saw that the cow was spraying dark fluid out of its back end, all over my lawn! This unwelcome beast had diarrhea and was relieving itself in my front yard! I had no idea what to do, so I yelled at it to F-off, clapping my hands loudly in an effort to shoo it away. I stomped out on the front deck, making continual assaulting noise, and it slowly ambled away, up the driveway, spraying its liquid fecal matter all over the place on its way. It wandered over toward the little cabins on the next property, and I thought, "Yeah, let them deal with it."

I went back into the house and back into the kitchen, totally pissed off that I had this irritating and disgusting "cleanup" in the yard to deal with before I could leave. Entering the kitchen, my eyes were drawn to the back yard, where at least ten more of the beasts, in all shapes and sizes, were grazing on my lawn and also dropping their feces all over the place! WTF!?!

Immediately, I knew where these cows had come from; that's right, Mr. Hobby Farmer behind me. I called his number and was so mad I left a brutal message saying, "Listen here, you better come and round up your livestock RIGHT NOW. If these cows aren't IMMEDIATELY removed from my yard, I'm going to put them in my freezer!" and then I went outside to deal with the unwelcome animals.

I was so mad that they must have understood that it was time to go by the tone and volume I was hollering at them in. They quickly exited my backyard, walking as fast as cows walk, into the front and then following my driveway out, toward the next property. But no, that's not where they went; uh-oh, they were going all the way out of my driveway and right out onto the incredibly busy highway! Immediately I could hear brakes and horns and screeching tires mixed with moos and other weird noises that cows make. Oops, LOL!

I ran into the house and dialed 911 and explained that there were a dozen cows on the highway and emergency response was needed to deal with this traffic disaster. And no, I didn't have any idea how they got on the highway (ha-ha!), but I knew who they belonged to and happily shared the info.

Yes, it turned out that the cows liked the hobby farmer as much as I did, and so they busted the fence and took a leave.

What a mess, AGAIN! A mess to me from that jerk who would, once again, not offer any apology or any compensation for the time it took me to restore my property after the incontinent stampede left. Imagine yourself as a guest staying at a B&B and waking up to this! Yes, your neighbors are a HUGE consideration—or concern, as the case may be—when you are operating a B&B.

· · · · ·

The Town

In a word, different.

In the large city that I moved from, I did all of my banking through the Internet, paid at the pump by shoving my card into a machine, and had food delivered by innocuous-looking teenagers in rusted-out Pintos. My mail was delivered while I was at work, so I couldn't tell you if the mailman was hot (it may not have been a man!), and someone would come and pick up my recycling and garbage. I never had to watch people make things happen for me in the sea of anonymity. Moving to the small town presented a new/old world where if you wanted something done, you had to take the project with you and see it done yourself. This means that you have to talk to people and watch them in action. I found this to be disturbing on most occasions.

In retrospect, I was never going to fit into that community. I was clearly from a big city, and that's not something you can hide; you look different, you talk different, your posture, experience, and habits are different, and they don't like it and they let you know it through the gossip-chain. By the time I was ready to sell the B&B and start a new life, I had pretty much cut myself off from the town. My very few good friends in town always said that you have to have a thick skin to live there, and that I should ignore the things they were saying and keep smiling. Having been the target of so many lies and so much hurtful gossip, I preferred my own company better than most people in town, so I spent most days alone enjoying the beauty and the serenity of my home and property. This was also, fortuitously, around the same time I began documenting these stories on my laptop.

All that Norman Rockwell stuff about the warm and welcoming small town? It's at least half bullshit.

. . . . .

The Citizen's "Arrest"

It's hard to move to a small town; you are not always welcomed, contrary to what you would expect from those visions that Norman Rockwell painted. As an outsider, I found that I was generally not welcomed or invited to be a part of the community, and that I was often treated very coolly, verging on just plain cold. Over many years, I only made a couple of really great friends—the kind that would invite me to their homes for personal occasions—and most of them moved away before I could finally leave the area for good. Of that tiny circle was a couple who had moved to the town from Europe also to purchase a B&B, and who also felt the icy cold treatment from many of the locals. One day over coffee, they told me a story that had them mortified; being foreigners and a little challenged with English and communication, they were even more frustrated, so they were requesting my help to react to the atrocity. Upon hearing the story, I was equally upset and didn't hesitate to write the following letter for them to submit to the Village Offices:

"My name is (name protected) and I have lived in (protected) for seven years, since my wife and I purchased (a local business). My family has worked hard both within our business but also for the betterment of the community, and none of us have any kind of a history that would warrant the behavior that I received last week from an employee of (Municipality).

On July 8, 2009, I had the job of taking the resort garbage to the dump around 9:00 or 10:00 a.m. When I arrived at the familiar place the gate was open, so I drove in and over to the garbage bins to deposit my bags. I put my bags in the bins and acknowledged the Village employees, who were also dumping from the big blue truck. I then got back into my truck and went to the metal area to leave a couple of small pieces of metal in the large area reserved for those products.

When I drove back toward the entrance, I saw that the gate had been closed and locked and on the other side of the fence was (dump employee, name protected), sitting in her truck. When she saw me approaching, she got out of her truck and walked over to the gate and began her extremely rude and angry prosecution of me, demanding to know what I was doing there and "how the hell" I got in here." I was completely stunned by her level of anger and suspicions, and I said, "What are you thinking? The gate was open, and I just drove in and was getting rid of my garbage." She fired back at me (still shouting) "It's Wednesday and you are not supposed to be in here," and she wanted to know how long I had been in there and how I got in there. I said, "I just told you, the gate was open and I just drove in here. I didn't realize that it's Wednesday."

I really didn't think about what day it was; when you have a resort business, every day is the same—people check in and people check out, you go to work every day, and your days off are rarely on a regular schedule. As a result, you are not always aware of what day it is, as there really aren't any indicators from your day-to-day operations to let you know that "today I cannot take my large pile of garbage to the dump because (for some reason that nobody seems to understand) it isn't open because it's Wednesday." Most people will agree with me; since this incident, I have shared this story with many people, all of whom replied that they had driven in to the dump only to discover that it was Wednesday and it was closed on more than one occasion.

Then I told her that there was also a truck from the Village with two ladies unloading garbage, so there was no way that I could *have realized that I was doing something wrong. Her response was that they were allowed to be there and that I was not, and neither was anybody else (I would like to know how she thinks THAT could have occurred to me?!). Then she threatened me with a fine of $10,000.00 because what I did was illegal and I could have contaminated the dump! I was shocked and insulted by the threat and the accusation, and I began to lose my patience and I said, "Come on, this is your neighbor you are talking to. Open the gate so I can leave, I have a lot of work to do today." She didn't stop yelling at me and lecturing me. I asked her a second time to open the gate and told her that I was not willing to listen to this bullshit anymore, but she refused and said that I had to stay there until I had taken her advice!! She, again, threatened me with the $10,000.00 fine and said that she could call the Regional District and restated that the Village was allowed to be here on Wednesday but not me or anybody else.*

Once again, I tried to plead my case and said that the gate was open and that it was not a crime if I go in there because I don't know it's Wednesday, and I asked her again to open the gate. She said no and told me that I have to listen to her and take her advice, so

I just stopped talking; clearly, it was hopeless to request a shred of leniency or neighborly compassion from this cantankerous and appallingly unprofessional person. Besides, what could I do? She had me locked in! And so I stood there for about another five minutes until she felt she had sufficiently unloaded her lecture on me and, finally, she opened the gate and ended my unwarranted incarceration.

This experience has been extremely upsetting for me not only because I am a just a customer who went to dump my garbage but also because this employee is a representative of the Regional District and her words and actions made me feel like the local authority was sending me a very hostile message. I didn't do anything wrong, as my only failing was not realizing that it was Wednesday. It was the same garbage that I would have dumped on Tuesday or Thursday, and there was nothing "illegal" about my actions or intentions, yet there I ended up jailed in the dump by an angry and unreasonable attendant. It was not a crime at all. I am not used to being treated like this; I have done nothing to even suggest to anyone that I am a criminal, yet that is exactly how I was treated.

I demand an apology from this employee and I also expect one from the Regional District on whose behalf she was acting. Her words and actions were nothing short of disgraceful. I think if employees are not able to do their job in a more professional capacity, and instead exhibit this kind of outrageous, embarrassing, and purely insulting behavior, then they should not have a job at all, especially one where they are a representative of not only the Regional District but also the Village of (protected) and the community.

Coincidentally (or maybe not really!), an hour or so after this, the Regional District representative came by in the company truck and paid a visit to my business. He slowly drove around, looking at the property very suspiciously to me. I felt like he was checking around my place, but I don't know why. It certainly felt like it was an extension of the experience earlier that morning and further solidified the message that was being sent to me. The Regional District representative then drove away without speaking to me at all.

I will expect an expedient response to this complaint and further consider my options in this matter.

Sincerely,

(name protected)"

Incidentally, my friends received an apology from the Municipality. That experience, for sure, will never be cleared from my friends' memories nor from the memories of their guests whose host was unable to assist with hosting while he was locked up at the dump.

·····

Beware the "ONE"-Town

Here's something to consider: ONE of anything in a small town is not great. What if the owner of a store is a greedy, mannerless asshole who you feel greatly ripped you off on more than one occasion? You can do one of two things: you can keep going there and let him think that he can get away with anything he feels like, or you can send a message by never stepping foot in there again, planning your trips to buy whatever you might need from that particular retailer in other towns or ordering it online. I chose the latter and didn't give him one more cent for at least two years that I lived in that valley. Sure, it cost me a little extra money and for sure more inconvenience, but was it worth it? Absolutely.

What if there's only one bank and the bank manager is incompetent, and the clerks spread personal banking information (like the salary of friend of mine!) around town? This was the state of affairs that I discovered not too long after I arrived. I was very pleased to see a turnaround as the years went by, but it was slow and it did mean that for a long time I had to expose my financial business to this institution and know that most of what was going on in my bank account was someone's coffee-talk.

One time, I was catering a giant wedding in the One-Town of a couple of nice locals that I knew pretty well. By this point, I had lived at the lodge for nearly eight (long and painful!) years. Because of the viewing schedule for a very short-notice potential buyer of my lodge, I had been unable to sneak out of town to make the giant dry-goods purchases that were going to be needed for a wedding of 250, so I had "sucked it up" and gone to the local grocery store to overpay for everything that I needed.

As I brought my $200 pile through the checkout, the cheery little new girl looked at me with big doe eyes and asked me why I was buying so much stuff. I told her that I was catering the local wedding that weekend. She then asked me why I didn't tell her so I could get the local business discount. I just about fainted. "WHAT local business discount are you talking about?" I inquired. "Oh, restaurants, B&Bs, and anyone doing a food service business gets 10% off everything in the store except dairy, so if you put the dairy at the end, we can apply the discount to everything before it." As Murphy's law would dictate, my dairy had all gone through first, so the discount could not be applied. The twenty bucks I could have saved that day pissed me off a bit, but nothing in comparison to how irate I felt when I thought about the amount of cash that I could have saved in the previous eight years of shopping there. Eight F-ing years of shopping there, and NOBODY had bothered to mention that little tidbit to me. They all knew who I was and which business I owned, and not once did anyone offer me the discount information, not even the manager.

Carefully consider the businesses that you value most and that you NEED to run your B&B, home, and life: the vet, the mechanic, the grocer, the bank, the hardware store, etc. Now think about what you'd do if they lost your trust, respect, and willingness to give them money. In a big city, it's of no consequence because you can go to the next guy. Now think about what you'd do if you don't have that option anymore.

. . . . .

Powerless

I've never realized how much I took a simple thing like electricity for granted until I moved to the small, remote town in the mountains. Before that time, power failures were so rare in my world that I never gave them a thought and they certainly didn't dictate my activities during a day, month, or season. But all that changed once I experienced the unreliable and archaic services that the small communities outside of the big cities receive from massive monopolizing companies that don't seem to give a damn about a small little thing called customer service. Winter power outages are the very worst because on acreage "no power" means "no power and no water

AND NO HEAT" and still, the power company would be unapologetic and, more or less, unsympathetic.

My first summer at the B&B was a real shocker where power was concerned. We had a power failure that began on the Friday of a major long weekend, and it lasted for six days in the small town, but for outlying properties like mine, it was ten full days. What was worse was that the big company was unhelpful in providing any information regarding when they might repair the problem, so nobody knew it would last as long as it did.

All the food in my refrigerator and freezers was destroyed, as was everyone else's. By the time everyone who didn't have a generator got one, it was too late. Restaurants lost so much inventory that they were financially devastated and a few never recovered. The motels in town could rent out rooms for guests to enjoy by candlelight. Since they were within the municipality, they had running water—so at least hygiene wasn't a concern. However, they still lost significant revenue, as they couldn't charge full price, and most travelers preferred to continue on to a community that offered full services.

For outlying properties like my own, it meant much worse. Because I was on a well, I had no power and no water either. TR brought a small generator out for the house, but it was in no way enough to operate as a B&B; I could plug in the TV to watch the news, and I could plug in one or two lights, but the water system was not available for the duration of the power outage. As well, it was a noisy gas motor, so it couldn't be operated for more than a couple of hours without driving you nuts and burning A LOT of gas. Obviously, I could not host guests in this environment, so not only did I lose a thousand dollars' worth of food but I also lost the revenue of that long weekend and had to turn both the booked-in guests and the drop-in guests away over those ten unpleasant days. I could use neither the toilets nor the shower and had to rely on friends with generators for these luxuries. It was extremely hot that summer also, so skipping the daily shower was definitely not an option.

Unfortunately, you can't always plan on the exact timing of your regular bodily functions, so as necessity is often the mother of invention, I quickly devised a hygienic system for the need to excrete. As the hot tub was also inoperable, there was a large body of unusable water sitting there and slowly becoming a bacterial hazard; it would have to be drained, sanitized, flushed, and refilled once the power came back on, so the water that was currently in it would have to be disposed of regardless of anything else. I could flush the toilets simply by pouring a large bucket of water into them; gravity works that way, so at least I could save a little dignity and "go" in a semi-civilized fashion.

After ten days it wasn't like the power came on and that was the end of it; there was another ten days of cleaning to be done, including vacuuming and washing of all floors, and serious cleaning of toilets, sinks, countertops, the fridge and freezers, and the hot tub. Because

I couldn't water my garden, there was a very substantial loss of veggies and that mess had to be cleaned up too. And all of this had to be done before I was able to have the go-ahead from the Health Inspector to take guests at the lodge again. All in all, it was one of the most unpleasant and frustrating things I had to endure to that point, but that was before the fire and the expulsion of TR from my life.

That was the longest power failure I experienced, but it certainly wasn't the only one. The power went out continually and for any reason you could think of. It got to the point where any time the wind blew beyond a light breeze, I would catch myself wondering if the power would go out.

. . . . .

One time, I was going skiing with friends who lived in the area and also owned an accommodation, but one that was much larger than my own. I drove to their property and we had a little visit inside and then we put on our gear and went outside. As we left the building, the power went out. That was the end of our plans. He had to work on getting their generator going and I had to hurry home to make the adjustments on the furnace and stay there to monitor the situation. Very disappointed, we went our separate ways.

When I got home, I discovered that my power was on, so I went inside and phoned to see if theirs had come on also. No, it hadn't yet—so it must've been a pretty localized outage that, for some reason, didn't affect me.

As I pondered this, I thought about what else I had to do that day; I had guests arriving that night and I was catering a large dinner the next night, so I had many things to pick up for these commitments. I was supposed to pick up the prime rib roast that I had ordered from the local grocer later that afternoon and had planned on doing that plus all of the shopping after the ski trip. A terrible thought s in my sparked in my brain: What if the power's out in town? The grocery store will close!

I quickly called the grocery store and was fortunate to have a friendly gal who worked there answer the phone, finding out that my feeling was dead-on and they were closed. I told her my dilemma, and she was extremely sympathetic and told me that she'd call me the second the power came on so I could come in and get my necessities. Then she told me that it would be up to ninety minutes, as she had been told by the power company. I was surprised that she had solid information like this so quickly, so I asked her if she knew the cause of the power failure. To my astonishment, she told me that a big fat crow had landed on a transformer in town, and both crow and transformer had blown up. "You're kidding!" was my shocked response. She calmly replied, "No, I'm not; someone here saw it happen, and I heard that the flash of light was as bright as a comet."

Wow. That's not something you'd ever experience in a big city; a store employee will call you to let you personally know when you can get in. I'm still a bit stunned from that one considering the countless stories of unpleasantness that I experienced, even just from that one business! The power did come back on sometime later, I was able to get my groceries, and by no further interventions of nature, the catering went off without further drama.

Over the fourteen years that I lived in that valley, the power continued to go out; it was definitely improved over that time with less frequent outages that lasted much shorter periods—but after experiencing the "early days," the concern was always there, and every so often we had a reminder that the power really could go out anytime.

· · · · ·

Chapter 9 - Reviews

Before opening yourself up to reviews, you had better thicken your skin - I, myself, have never been very good at that. I always took a HUGE amount of pride in my hosting, my home, my yard, and my ability to materialize proverbial magic for my guests. As I write this paragraph, years later, I know I haven't evolved at all in that respect. I take pride in anything to do with customer experience, whether it be friends and family in my home for dinner or an extended stay or the services that I extend to my clients in my current business. I'm as sensitive as anyone and I've always felt mortally wounded by a really negative comment. Very harsh criticism is like tearing a muscle for me; it takes a while to heal and I'm conscious of the event for a long, long time. If this is how you are too, I suggest you find a good outlet for venting those frustrations, because freaking out and telling the online reviewer that they're an idiot is probably not the best solution.

Airbnb came along in the early 2000's, and I joined a couple of years into my Bed & Breakfast stint. I was one of the first to join in my area, but was soon followed by a plethora of local "rentals" who ranged in their offerings from bad to ridiculous—it seemed like anyone with a spare room was joining in to bring the bar down for those of us who were running respectable B&Bs.

I thought the Airbnb system worked well for me; it had a few hiccups, but all in all I liked it. I especially liked the idea of me being able to review my guests and not just them reviewing me, my home, and the experience they went away with. I felt like that system would keep them from acting like barbarians in my home and it would also keep their reviews "real." For the most part, I was right about that, but every so often I was surprised by what I came to call "bullshit reviews" by self-appointed swords of justice who were going to expose all the evil truths with the aid of their "expertise." It seemed like some folks were possessed by the traveling spirits of Anthony Bourdain or Gordon Ramsay, and felt it their sworn duty to find something, no matter how inconsequential, to pick apart and literally create a mountain out of a molehill.

There were a surprising number of reviewers who took points off for location, of all things! Before you judge, you need to know that the location was very specifically shown on a Google map and described in-depth in the write-up, so for anyone to be unhappy about the location was ridiculous.

I once had a couple visit from Calgary, Alberta; if memory serves correctly, they were celebrating an anniversary. They were booked in for three nights during the summer and the weather was perfect. Everything was perfect as far as I could tell: the breakfasts all turned out beautifully, and they ate under the big umbrella on the back deck, which was the perfect place to enjoy the yard and sun which provided a perfect summer experience for their entire stay. They enjoyed their days, touring around, seeing sights, small hikes, a day-trip to the National Park nearby, and evenings with the TV, a glass of wine on a deck, or reading in their room. The best part was that they were the only people that had booked in at that time, so they had the entire common area, parking, the entire property, and everything all to themselves.

When they left, I expected a near-perfect review, but that is not what came; amongst other BS was *"The bathroom is shared with other guests and is not huge."* I thought, "Are you kidding? Who the F did you share the bathroom with, your imaginary friends?" I immediately responded that there was no sharing of bathrooms, and if another couple or guest would have booked in, I would have put them on the other floor so that each party would have their own private bathroom. And their comments on the bathroom being small? It was a standard bathroom with a five-foot counter, sink, two cupboards, six drawers, a toilet, a full-size bathtub with shower, and ample towel racks, etc. It was stocked with all the shampoos, body washes, soaps, toothpaste, blow-dryer and even disposable razors, cotton swabs, and pads that they wanted to use. The exact measurements of this bathroom were five feet, four inches deep and nine feet long; the same size as any other average bathroom. Apparently, the bathroom size is a big deal for fulfilling their laundry list of things to write bullshit reviews on.

· · · · ·

Here are actual reviews, verbatim, cut and pasted with no edits:

Public feedback

What a lovely gem of a spot! The lodge provided a great place to relax and explore the area. The space itself is beautiful with a large common area, great hot tub to soak in and beautiful surroundings. Sue was a gracious host and an excellent resource. She created a fantastic meal each morning and was open to adapt to our dietary needs—all the food was delicious!! Sue also gave us great places to check out in the area. The beds were super comfortable, the lodge incredibly clean and was centrally located to many local attractions. This was a great place for a getaway and would recommend it to those coming to this area.

· · · · ·

Private feedback

-having a microwave for guests to use if they could like to heat up a small meal while visiting

-inquire into how much space and interaction guests would like with host upon arrival

Really? Don't people understand "B&B" concept? It stands for Bed and Breakfast, which you got. You don't get to cook your own food in my beautiful home; this is against Public Health rules. And as for interaction, if you didn't want the host to be around, you should have booked that private little hotel room—you know the one, it's the one that's got a microwave in it!

. . . . .

Public feedback

Our stay at the (Name of my lodge) in the Canadian Rockies was a great experience. The place is really nice—indoor as well as outdoor. The host is welcoming and service-minded and a great host. Everything was to our likings, and the included breakfast was a treat unexpected. Sue went out of her way to cook us outstanding breakfasts, and the overall place was in line with that. The location to the National Park is doable, but longer than we had planned for. The place can be used as a hub to visit the National Park, but one should be aware of the time spent in transport. However, if the purpose is to enjoy the Rockies in general combined with great hospitality and beautiful settings, it is definitely worth a visit.

Yes, generally a good review, except for that nonsense in the middle that it was farther from the National Park than they had expected. Come on now, dude!

You found my site using a computer that probably has Google, where you could have found out exactly how far that Park was from my lodge. Oh, wait a minute, you didn't even have to work that hard because there was a Google map right on my Airbnb listing showing you exactly where that Park is in proximity. I suppose you could have checked my website too, because there was a Google map on there too showing you exactly where my lodge was and gave distances to all points of interest, including the National F-ing Park. Failing all else, you could have asked me how far that Park was and I would have simply told you. By the way, if you wanted to spend your vacation in the National Park, why didn't you book a B&B there? Oh, that's right, it would have cost you a load more cash, which is why you booked my place, isn't it? So, we can surmise that you did and had all the research, you chose to pay less, travel more, and make it my fault. Thanks.

· · · · ·

Public feedback

Sue has a well-run B&B which is spotless and spacious. She is obviously experienced and very friendly. Her breakfasts were generous and ready when we were. She was very helpful with information and made phone calls for us to set up meals, etc. She was very responsive with communication and all her instructions were clear and kind. Great spot to get to Mount Robson and the Lake Kinney hike, which is breathtaking!

.....

Private feedback

This is just for you. It won't appear on your listing or profile.

Beds a bit saggy in the middle.

This was an incredibly overweight couple (that came up in a previous story); they could have slept on an actual mountain and it would have sagged in the middle.

.....

Public feedback

Very welcoming, best breakfast EVER! Great relaxing in the hot tub after a strenuous hike…could not be beat.

This review was interesting to me. There were three couples, most of whom were polite, but all were very dismissive to me; they did not invite me to visit with them or even ask my advice on anything about the area. One of the three men was beyond rude to me, going out of his way to insult me on several occasions, even finding many faults with their lovely breakfasts. The wives were also quite unpleasant, looking down their noses at me and not friendly at all, making me walk on eggshells around them and get far out of their way the second my breakfast responsibilities were over. I felt hurt by them by the end of their stay; I was glad to see them leave after having been treated like a servant to them. They seemed so snooty and unimpressed that I expected a bad review but got that instead; it pissed me off reading it, as I felt that I deserved better treatment while they stayed.

As I said, with Airbnb you get to review each other, and neither of you gets to read the other's comments until you have both submitted your reviews. I was honest with my review of them, reiterating all of what I said in the last paragraph, to which I received absolutely no response.

. . . . .

Public feedback

Wow, what a beautiful place! We all loved staying at Sue's place and will surely come back. The breakfasts are a daily feast and so delicious, Sue is a top chef. The rooms are great, bedding very comfortable, and the private bathrooms equipped with more than ample the amenities. The garden is a dream and beautiful manicured. Sue is the perfect host at all times and has a great sense of humour. We look forward to staying at her lodge in the near future.

No BS on this public feedback; this was cut and pasted word for word. Clearly, I had very worldly and extremely wise travelers! (I felt like I had to include at least one truly great review, and yes, there were many more of them than the lousy ones!) Please note that she mentions both private bathrooms and comfortable beds.

·····

Chapter 10 - Reservations Required

People have no respect for your time or privacy when you operate a B&B. They think that you are just sitting there waiting for them to show up; that you have no other thing that weighs as important as them dropping into your life at their convenience. It never failed to surprise me how often this rang true, as time and time again I was surprised by guests without a confirmation or booking.

I remember once, a friend and I were sitting in the hot tub in the backyard. It was in the evening, after dinner, and we were having a couple of drinks and relaxing, enjoying the peace and quiet of the place with no guests that evening. Without any notice, around the corner a family comes wandering into my back yard. They had gone to the front door, knocked and received no answer, so they tried the door handle, and having no success with that either, they decided to go look for a back door and instead found us lounging in the private back yard. It shocked me that they would be so brazen as to go on a search to get into a private home in the darkening hours of a fall evening without giving me any notice to expect them.

These sorts of things happened often; so often that there are too many of them to recount and they would bore you to death because they're all exactly like the last one. Proprietor has no bookings, decides to take "me" time, gets caught by unannounced guest in an awkward position—usually either in pajamas, in the hot tub, or in the middle of hosting an elaborate dinner party for a few close friends. At this point, it's pertinent to add that it doesn't matter what your vacancy sign says, either!

There's one other story worth recalling. It encompasses all the problems of the B&B, the bad neighbors, and the disrespectful non-bookers, so it pissed me off and irritated the heck out of me for a long, LONG time.

One weekend, I got a phone call from a young woman who worked for a friend of mine in town the year before. I hadn't heard a thing of her since, so I thought she may have moved on; she wasn't a "local" and she seemed like the type to pick up and go whenever the mood struck. She owned next to nothing and she seemed to be guided by whatever her current boyfriend had to offer her. I had only had a couple of conversations with her but was definitely not impressed by anything she had to offer to those exchanges. Get the picture?

Her father was coming to visit, and she was looking for options for places for him to stay and trying to find out the prices. I asked her when he was coming, and she said she thought it was that Wednesday or Thursday. Then I asked her how long he was staying, and she didn't really know; it all seemed to be very vague. I quoted her a low rate, as she was a local neighbor in a bind with no extra space for her dad to stay. She said that she'd call back to let me know what she decided, and I didn't hear back from her at all, so it was out of my thoughts: no booking.

By Tuesday morning, I had made plans with a couple of good friends to go to their place for lovely antipasti and wines on Wednesday at 4:00 p.m. I knew it would be a few hours because we always found lots to talk about and shared many great passions, including fine food and wine, and never rushed any of them when we had our get-togethers.

So, before I headed to their place, I had forwarded my B&B phone line to my cell phone, as I always did when I left the property. It was my feeling that an answering machine wasn't as good an option as having the phone professionally answered and the call dealt with as it happened. Thinking back, I should have developed a policy not to answer any calls from local numbers that I did not recognize and let them leave a message. Sadly, I didn't do that when my cell phone rang at around 4:30 p.m. and we were just starting on a lovely Italian prosecco with an array of sensational finger foods.

It was the little lady. "Hi, Sue, it's me, ___. My dad's here, so I'm going to bring him over now." I was a bit stunned, saying "You didn't call me back to confirm, I had no idea he would be arriving, and I'm not even there right now." Silence. "Listen, ___, I have made other plans for this evening and can't help you until tomorrow." "Oh, well," she said, "I'll talk to my dad and see what he wants to do." Then the call ended.

My friends were appalled by her actions but not surprised. Having also moved to that area to own and operate a tourist accommodation business, they were more than familiar with this disrespectful and imposing behavior. We all shook our heads and moved on with our indulgences.

The next morning, I woke up and was still irritated at the young lady's insolence, especially since I still didn't know if or when her dad might show up and at which time it might convenience her to let me know those little details. I called her back at the number that she called me from to find out what her plans were. When she answered the phone, I explained to her that when she didn't confirm, I had not expected them and turned out to be unavailable for her father's arrival the evening before, and now was wondering whether she would be bringing him by that day and at what time. She replied that he had gotten a room at a motel in town and would stay there, so they would not be coming to my place. And so, with no booking, the call was ended and I was left with the feeling that this whole episode would end up translated to it being "my fault."

Immersed in my various chores a while later, I looked up to see a woman walking up my steps. She knocked on the door and I answered it. It was the traveling companion of the father of the local girl wondering when they could move in (I was NEVER informed that there would be two guests). I told her that the girl had told me this morning that they had found somewhere else to stay and would not be staying with me. I also told her that I didn't even know they had planned to stay at my place until the night before, when the girl called me to announce the arrival. I explained to her that there was supposed to be a confirmation and there was not, and that because I had no expectation of guests, I had made other plans and left the property and was unavailable when they first arrived. She gave me a small smile, like she wanted to end it on a pleasant note, said goodbye, and left.

At that moment, I KNEW this experience was going to be translated to "proprietor's fault, what a bitch." Whatever. I knew I could have made the choice to have taken the high road and let them stay, but at the end of the day I was already past the point of giving a damn what the locals had to say about me. I also told myself that I saved myself the next few days of uncomfortable living due to hillbillies hanging around and disrespecting both me and my home. At the time, my place had been on the market for several months, and at that moment, I yearned for the day that my B&B would be sold and that I would be leaving the business and the area forever.

· · · · ·

Ridiculous Reservation Requests

People don't give enough thought to what they are proposing, and sometimes you feel the urge to hit them with a bit of sarcasm to bounce them back into reality. I did not book in any of the following people because, as you'll see, they were WAY over the line.

"Hello, I'd like to make a reservation for two couples."

"Great." We chatted as I took the details of their stay, and over the course of the conversation, it became clear that their activity schedule would keep them away from the house for a minimum of eight hours during the daytimes, as they were coming up to do some serious snowmobiling.

"We're bringing our dogs with us; two are small and one is larger, but they're really good and they won't be a bother to you at all while we're out."

Unbelievable! He actually thought he could bring three dogs into a private home with a commercially licensed kitchen and expect the owner to dog-sit for him all day while they were out having a good time. Right! I have nothing better to do! After I got rid of him, I made a few calls to local accommodations to see if they would allow this for future consideration, and guess what? Nobody would; surprise, surprise!

. . . . .

"Hello, I'd like to reserve the whole place for three couples and three children."

"Great! When would you like to arrive?"

"December 23rd, and stay until the 28th."

"OK, would you like the Bed & Breakfast package or the All-Meals package?"

"Oh, we don't need you to make any meals; in fact, we want the whole place to ourselves with nobody else there, and we'll cook our own meals."

Unbelievable! He thought he could boot me out of my own home for Christmas and let him and his family run amuck through my place and possessions. And he thought he could cook his meals IN MY PRISTINE KITCHEN that's commercially licensed (like a restaurant) under the Health Board!

I felt like telling him to reverse the situation in his own head, think about it for a few days, and call me back to apologize for being such a dumbass!

· · · · ·

Here's a good one from my first fall in the business:

"Hi, we're coming out to do some hunting. Can we use your shop to bleed the animals?"

Unbelievable! (Not to mention SO F-ING DISGUSTING!!!)

PS: Thanks pal; you just made me throw up on my phone!

· · · · ·

One day I answered a call from a stranger:

"Hi, do you have any availability for next weekend?" To finish his request, he burped loudly in my ear over the phone.

What do you think? You will not be stepping foot in my home.

· · · · ·

Chapter 11 - Selling the B&B

It took a long time to sell the B&B. It's not a business that a bank will touch, particularly in a world recession (listed during the crash of 2007-2008). The guests, reservations, and money are not guaranteed, so banks have no faith in debt repayment. Essentially, what this means is that when you sell, you have to wait for the buyer who has a giant down payment for the bank or, ideally, the full amount in cash.

This can be a frustrating thing to wait for. You think you have a buyer; they contact you, they come to view (sometimes more than once), they basically tell you to "start packing" (and like an idiot, you do), then the offer comes in and you are reeling in shock because it's 40% down from where you want to be. Later, the agent will explain that it was all the money they could get, so they made the offer hoping you were desperate enough to take it.

Or then there are the guys who try to pull every bit of wool from the sheep over your eyes…

I got a call from a guy who was interested in the property and wanted to add an RV park and make a few other changes to improve the business. Great, do whatever you like; try to remember that I'm selling; aka LEAVING, WALKING AWAY, DON'T CARE WHAT HAPPENS HERE AFTER I GO! I DON'T GIVE A DAMN ABOUT YOUR FUTURE PLANS FOR THIS HOME OR PROPERTY; TRY NOT TO BORE ME WITH THE DETAILS.

At first, he wanted to do what he called "some horse-trading." He would get my fantastic, developed, landscaped property in the middle of the BC Rockies with a million-dollar log home on it and a million-dollar view, and I would get a couple of pieces of undeveloped swamp in rural Alberta. I'm sure you're saying to yourself, "What a great deal, why didn't you take it?" LOL, I have to say it was hard to maintain my diplomacy when faced with the suggestion.

Once I explained to him that I would not be interested in that scenario, he blew it off and continued the negotiations, bragging about his money, his business, and how this was a great thing for him and his company. I googled him (I google everybody, it's awesome what you can find out through the internet!) and discovered that he just may have been a guy who had the means to make this happen: real company, seemed successful, and certainly talked the real talk. I must admit that I got a bit caught up in his potential value and so when he came out with his "marketing guy," I didn't charge them for their stay. At no point did he offer to pay, and since he bought me dinner in town after his arrival, I (overgenerously, as usual) didn't bother to make up a bill. Then, a couple of weeks later he came out with his "business partner," and again, I didn't charge them.

Then I didn't hear from him for a month. Somewhere inside I knew that I had been duped by a slick dude in a nice car. At least I was braced for the response that I got from him when I contacted him to find out what was happening with our negotiations:

"Thanks for the email and I am off the radar to purchase your lodge as it is really hard to get the banks to lend on your type of building as a business."

Note to self: YOU STAY, YOU PAY; I DON'T CARE IF YOU'RE DONALD TRUMP (I used to love "the Donald," as he seemed like a cool dude—that is until he decided to give up reality TV shows and run for President!) AND HAVE THE CASH IN YOUR CAR, YOU'RE GIVING ME YOUR CARD UP FRONT AND THE RATE WILL BE EXACTLY AS YOU SEE IT ON MY WEBSITE. If you buy the place, I'll happily reimburse you, but I suspect that if you are serious and you have enough money to buy this place, you will likely not be the guy who tries to stay for free.

. . . . .

I made a policy that "buyers" were no longer welcome to stay in my home and that's when I discovered how deceitful people could be to get in the door. A long weekend was upcoming, and I received a call from a guy who wanted to know if he could book in for the long weekend. I told him that I was sorry, but I had no availability at that time for him. He took a long pause then asked me how many rooms I had, like he was challenging my statement a little. I told him that I had four guest rooms with two beds in each room. He took another long pause, then said, "I see you're selling out." Busted! This dude was a buyer posing as a customer. "Yes, I am," was my simple response; for trying to snow me, I would not be volunteering any extra info. "So, are you selling or are you looking for investors?" Are you kidding me? How many people get investors to invest in their home? Clearly not too bright, but that didn't necessarily mean that he didn't have the dough to seal the deal. "No, I'm selling out entirely, moving forward so to speak." "Well, we wanted to check it out while we were staying there, so maybe we'll just drop by to see the place." (Are you high? You can't pull into a private lodge where showings are BY APPOINTMENT ONLY, as is clearly indicated on the website you are looking at!!) "Well, that will not really work if there are guests here, you see, as they do have an expectation of privacy, so it's not like you can take a tour while they're either here or have their belongings trusted to safety in a private lodge." "What about the Monday? Can we drop in that day?" "It depends if they've left or not, as well. I plan showings for when the place is clean. The best thing to do is to call ahead and make an appointment for when there are no guests here;

it's not possible for me to show the place when there's a full house of guests on an all-meals booking." Clearly this guy had no idea how much work is involved in this business—which would make him ideal to buy it!

The long weekend came and went, and my big group left late on the Monday. Most of my day was spent trying to make the place as presentable as possible because buddy was "dropping by," likely without any phone call first. I cleaned the great room (kitchen, bar, living room) and stripped beds, but couldn't do bathrooms or floors as the guests were coming back to shower, pack, and pay before leaving. All day long I stressed over the place being too dirty to show, but you can probably guess what happened—he never showed up at all.

. . . . .

Selling a public accommodation invites a world of wackos into your life. These days, everything is accessible over the internet and so you have inquiries coming in from everywhere and from every kind of person. From the online advertisements I received countless inquiries and quickly formed a detail-packed cut and paste response that I just sent off to everyone. If they responded back, then I would begin a unique dialogue with them covering the additional information that they requested. This one sticks out as one of the most outrageous responses I received; try to keep a straight face!

"From: Capt David West
[mailto:captdavidwest@gmail.com]

Sent: Sunday, December 12, 2010 8:37 AM
To:
Subject: Confidential
Dear Sue,
I am Captain David West and i am a member of NATO-ISAF Task Force and Provincial Reconstruction Troops in Southern Afghanistan.I am interested in the property,i am a private buyer and want to buy the property for my family use,in line with my business and family interest in your country,i have a very confidential proposal for you.

Based on the USA legislative and executive decision of pulling our troop out of here, i have decided to contact you for this business opportunity and relationship.I want to inform you that I have in my possession the sum of USD 11.5 million, which I got from crude oil deals in Iraq.I deposited this money with a Red Cross Agent informing him that i am making contact for the real owner of the money and it is under my power to approve whoever comes forth for the money.

I want to invest the money in a good business as soon as my service here ends,anyway you will advice me on that since I am not a business person.I am solely interested in making a life for my two daughters and therefore i shall require the service of a person who is trustworthy and sincere and i am going to make you the beneficiary of the money and allowing you to invest for my Kids in the event anything happens to me here.I am an American and an intelligence officer, so I have a 100% authentic means of transferring the money through diplomatic courier service.I just need your acceptance and all is done.

Where we are now we can only communicate through our military communication facilities that are secured so nobody can monitor our emails, then I can explain in details to you. I will only reach you through email, because our calls might be monitored, I just have to be sure whom I am dealing with.

I need someone I could deal with on trust, so that is why i contacted you to work with me as the receiving partner in your country. If you accept, I will put you forward as the beneficiary of the funds and transfer the money to you because as a uniformed person I cannot be parading such an amount so I need to present someone as the beneficiary.

I am writing from a fresh email account so if you are not interested do not reply to this email and please delete this message.

> *If you are interested, then let me know so we can proceed as time is very important to me. In less than five days, the money should have been in your position and I will come over for my money. I will give to you 30% of the sum and 70% is for me because I know that nothing goes for nothing, I hope I am been fair to you for your assistance as my receiving partner.*
> *Get back to me urgently, if you are interested in this business deal.*
> *Kind regards,*
> *Capt David West"*

Can you believe this? I was stunned that someone could be so crass as to try to pull such crap over on me!

My response:

> LOL!!! You've got to be kidding! Not interested in the BS you're trying to sell, "Captain."
> Have a nice day, thanks for bringing us a good laugh.
> Don't bother contacting me again either.

. . . . .

Here's a head-scratcher:

> *Dear Sir/Madam,*
> *I am very interested in buying your business.*
> *My lender requires historic trading figures including statutory and management accounts*

> *for the past three years in order to finance the purchase.*
> *Please would you provide these?*
> *Cedric.*

WTF does that even mean? Clearly Cedric thinks that I'm selling the World Trade Center. Dude, it's a B&B; it's really not that complicated.

. . . . .

One cold morning in the middle of Christmas break, I was settling into my between-guests routine of savoring designer coffee and looking over emails in my office, wearing my pajamas. It was 8:55 a.m., I had just poured my second cup, and the phone rang. I checked the caller ID and didn't recognize the 780-area code number, so I answered with my professional voice.

The voice on the other end was a harsh, abrasive woman who was in desperate need of telephone-manner-school. She wanted to view my place and she had been "trying and trying to reach the girls at the office here to arrange this" and so they want to come now, in twenty minutes. I was a bit fuzzy still and a bit confused by her comments. I asked her what girls she was referring to, as my realtor was a male out of Kelowna whose direct cell phone number was published on all advertising relating to the sale. She rudely blew off my question and again stated that they wanted to come right away. I agreed, hung up the phone, and headed to my suite to find clothes and a bit of makeup.

Ten minutes later, they were pulling into the driveway. Fortunately, I had moved quickly so I had my hair in a ponytail, a bit of nice fresh paint on, a squirt of Calvin Klein, and was just zipping up the fly on my jeans when I heard the knock on the door. I went downstairs, glued on my hostess-with-the-mostess smile, and opened the door while extending my hand to introduce myself as the owner.

He surrendered his hand and a weak smile, but she offered to only stare a hole through my head with no sign of pleasantness. I immediately felt empathy for the dude; it must be a bit sad to go through life with a woman who not only wears the pants but a Kevlar suit and an iron mask to go with it, yuck.

Without any thought, I moved into my "impossible customer" response: kind, polite, sweet, friendly, funny, adorable, and calm. That's going to be funny to anyone who knows me because I'm a Taurus and that is (to say the least) a bit of a stretch for us. The thing is you can't please that person, so there's nothing left to do but irritate them further by killing them with kindness. If you do the full psych-circle you get it—it actually is very "Taurus" to be able to pull the strength together to turn on this personality for the sole purpose of torturing a jerk.

With big doe eyes and a soft voice, I asked her again whom she was trying to "get hold of". Once again, she only gave me part of an answer and wanted to change the subject. I could tell by the response and her eyes that were averted from me that she was either lying or had no clue what she was talking about—and it wouldn't take long for me to find out which.

We began the tour but she didn't seem to want to be there at all. She barely stepped into rooms, and not at all into a few of them, and carried her "smart" phone (this is such an oxymoron when you think about it) around in her hand, continually texting and fiddling that made it keep beeping throughout our walk. Her rudeness caused me to shift all comments to the dude alone, who was the only one of them that was respecting my time and my tour information about various steps of the construction that had been completed four years previous.

She interrupted my banter with a comment that they were only interested in having it as a vacation home. I recognized this ploy from previous "buyers"; this meant, "I want it all but if I tell you that the business part of it doesn't interest me then I may be able to get it for way less money." Fat chance. First of all, it's a package; you can't tell me that you want the house and business but don't like the property, so you shouldn't have to pay for the property either—it is what it is and you can buy it or you can go away and quit annoying me. Second of all, and once again, what you do with it when you buy it is none of my business; DON'T BORE ME WITH THE DETAILS. So, I gave her the same response that she gave me. I blew it off, didn't respond at all, then I continued sweetly showing the poor dude around while ignoring the bulldog behind us.

She didn't like to be ignored, so she shot another comment in at the end of the inside part of the tour, "It's for my uncle, who just wants it for a vacation home." "Really? Why isn't he here?" was my response (half sarcastically, I might add). "He's in Malaysia right now." I couldn't put the filters "on" fast enough, so with a hearty laugh I said, "Well, I guess I won't hold my breath for the deposit cheque right away!" I instantly had part of my answer; by the chuckle that creeped out of the nice dude, I knew without any doubt that she was lying about something. As she tossed him a death-stare, I changed the subject by asking them if they had any questions; with a crossed brow, she demanded to know when the last time it had been inspected was. Now I had the rest of my answer; she didn't know what the hell she was talking about, obviously had never built a house and gone through the hoops with the building inspector, and likely had never bought or sold a house either. Again, the filters didn't turn on fast enough, so I sarcastically asked her "Why would I inspect it? I built it and had the building inspector approve every step along the way." Apparently, his filters weren't fast enough either and he let out another chuckle that was quickly smothered by another death-stare. Wow, I thought, she's going to kick the shit out of him later, poor dude.

It was then time to do the outside tour, which she opted out of in a very dismissive manner to make a phone call over by their vehicle, and so I showed the dude around the garage, shop, property lines, and gave him a bit of info on the adjacent properties. We chatted a bit; he was nice, experienced enough to understand everything that I told him, and I got the sense that he was much more honest than his counterpart.

We had completed the tour, and she had completed her phone call, joined us on the front sidewalk, and announced that she had reconfirmed that her uncle in Malaysia wanted it as a vacation home only but wanted a brochure or something they could take away. I gave her my realtor's card with all of his contact information and explained that every bit of info was on his website, it was also available through the online MLS (she didn't know what that was—further confirmation that she didn't know what the hell she was doing), and also on the international business website that it was advertised on. She said her uncle didn't have internet access where he was. This time I turned the filters on before the obvious comment came out (So, you can randomly call him on the phone from the middle of the mountains to an undisclosed location in "Malaysia," but yet he has no access to the internet? Come on now, you're making yourself look like a bad liar now!). I smoothly replied that she could email my realtor and he could mail her anything she liked to anywhere in the world.

I could tell she hated me and I didn't care. Not only did she not win whatever stupid little game she was trying to play with me, but I managed to get her to show all of her true colours and all three of us knew it; it was out there and nobody could take it back.

Later that day when I relayed the events to my realtor, I told him that I hoped that this would be the last we would hear from this bunch. I also gave him her cell phone number from my caller ID and instructed him to call her one or two or fifty times to follow up, as she clearly thought it was OK to impose.

. . . . .

Here's another good example of imposition:

Two days before a Thanksgiving weekend, I receive an email from a woman who asked to come for a showing with her husband on the Sunday of the long weekend. I thought it was odd; don't they have things to do on Thanksgiving? Don't they think I might too? How imposing! But I thought to myself, "more important to sell the place than to judge buyers on their lack of holiday rituals", so I emailed her back telling her that would be fine, I would be there and available for them from 10:00 a.m. to 4:00 p.m. that day.

I was very excited to see them; I hated the thought of another winter with another season of people in my house who I'd bust my ass trying to make happy; some with success, some not so much. By this point, I was pretty desperate to sell and had lowered the price to 20% below the assessment value. Any opportunity to unload the place was like the proverbial light at the end of the tunnel.

I spent all day Friday and Saturday cleaning nooks and crannies, making everything perfect for them. The weather was nasty, lots of rain and wind, but it promised to clear up for Sunday, which was ideal for the showing; a place always looks better in the sun, plus you have the bonus of the mountains in the surrounding view!

Sunday was beautiful, sunny and calm as promised. Everything was perfect, from the manicured lawn to the immaculately weeded flower and vegetable gardens and throughout the interior of the building. At 10:00 a.m. I was already pacing with nervous excitement, by noon I had bit every fingernail off, and by 2:00 p.m. I was manic and wondering why they were so late! When 4:00 p.m. hit, I was pissed off. They simply destroyed that Thanksgiving for me by making me wait around for them ALL DAY; they did not show up, didn't call, didn't email, and I would not hear from them again. Unbelievable.

. . . . .

A fellow once contacted me, supposedly from South Africa and desperate to buy my lodge. He owned a spa in South Africa that had a sale pending on it, but it was a bit of a complicated sale, blah-blah-blah. It was all by email; as he awaited his money for the sale, he and I were in contact frequently over a period of a couple of years, by which time I had more or less concluded that he was either never going to get there or was a straight-up liar and completely wasting my time. I had googled him and for sure he did work there, at that spa in South Africa, but it was impossible to know if he was the owner or not.

To my surprise, after a long period of not hearing from him he emailed me to say that he was arriving the next day! And he did! And he was definitely South African and driving an expensive car. He checked out the whole place, asked many questions, and informed me that yes, he had received all of his money and was now able to buy my lodge. "What the F? Is this really happening to me?" I silently asked myself. We agreed on a price and he said he would be back the following week with his realtor and all documents.

I never heard from him again. Asshole.

I googled one day the following year and guess where I found him? He was on LinkedIn and a waiter in Vancouver. Just to be facetious, I messaged him on that site and congratulated him on his new job.

. . . . .

"What chattels are included?"

I had to google that one before responding, LOL!

. . . . .

Sometimes it's hard to believe they even found your listing:

> "you called me back regarding my interest of your business sorry i missed you can you forward me more info on the property pitchers of all rooms ect
>
> and send you financial statements from the last five years, additional information

if you need me to sine a non-disclosure agreement can you send it to this e-mail

kind regards..." [sic]

Seriously? If I were a bank, I wouldn't give you a cheque book. Go back to school, learn spelling, punctuation, and grammar, then send me an email that makes sense.

· · · · ·

There were so many inquiries over the years I couldn't possibly get them all down and you might get pissed off reading them all. The final word is that the place finally did sell—to a couple who were both close to my age when TR and I bought it. They were enthusiastic, optimistic, and could not wait to begin "living the dream." They had grand ideas for changes and improvements and whenever I drive by their property, I see that they have changed, added and subtracted elements… which doesn't make me feel anything. I wish them well with their endeavors and I hope their hosting dreams are all coming true after buying my beautiful home…. but there's a nagging feeling deep inside me that says it's probably not at all what they thought it would be.

· · · · ·

About the Author

With a career in customer service, the author spent fourteen unforgettable years running a B&B lodge in the stunning Canadian Rockies. When she's not recounting her wild B&B tales, she enjoys golf, boating, hiking, biking, skiing, gym workouts, and indulging in a glass of good wine. Now residing in British Columbia's picturesque Okanagan Valley, she continues to embrace the great outdoors and all the adventures life has to offer.

Sue invites very few guests to her home these days.

www.ingramcontent.com/pod-product-compliance
Lightning Source LLC
LaVergne TN
LVHW090326120126
829601LV00009B/504